Editor-in-Chief and Founder:
Lyndon H. LaRouche, Jr.
Editorial Board: *Lyndon H. LaRouche, Jr. , Helga
Zepp-LaRouche, Robert Ingraham, Tony
Papert, Gerald Rose, Dennis Small, Jeffrey
Steinberg, William Wertz*
Co-Editors: *Robert Ingraham, Tony Papert*
Managing Editor: *Nancy Spannaus*
Technology: *Marsha Freeman*
Books: *Katherine Notley*
Ebooks: *Richard Burden*
Graphics: *Alan Yue*
Photos: *Stuart Lewis*
Circulation Manager: *Stanley Ezrol*

INTELLIGENCE DIRECTORS
Counterintelligence: *Jeffrey Steinberg, Michele
Steinberg*
Economics: *John Hoefle, Marcia Merry Baker,
Paul Gallagher*
History: *Anton Chaitkin*
Ibero-America: *Dennis Small*
Russia and Eastern Europe: *Rachel Douglas*
United States: *Debra Freeman*

INTERNATIONAL BUREAUS
Bogotá: *Miriam Redondo*
Berlin: *Rainer Apel*
Copenhagen: *Tom Gillesberg*
Houston: *Harley Schlanger*
Lima: *Sara Madueño*
Melbourne: *Robert Barwick*
Mexico City: *Gerardo Castilleja Chávez*
New Delhi: *Ramtanu Maitra*
Paris: *Christine Bierre*
Stockholm: *Ulf Sandmark*
United Nations, N.Y.C.: *Leni Rubinstein*
Washington, D.C.: *William Jones*
Wiesbaden: *Göran Haglund*

ON THE WEB
e-mail: eirns@larouchepub.com
www.larouchepub.com
www.executiveintelligencereview.com
www.larouchepub.com/eiw
Webmaster: *John Sigerson*
Assistant Webmaster: *George Hollis*
Editor, Arabic-language edition: *Hussein Askary*

EIR (ISSN 0273-6314) *is published weekly
(50 issues), by EIR News Service, Inc.,
P.O. Box 17390, Washington, D.C. 20041-0390.
(703) 297-8434*

European Headquarters: E.I.R. GmbH, Postfach
Bahnstrasse 9a, D-65205, Wiesbaden, Germany
Tel: 49-611-73650
Homepage: http://www.eir.de
e-mail: info@eir.de
Director: Georg Neudecker

Montreal, Canada: 514-461-1557
eir@eircanada.ca

Denmark: EIR - Danmark, Sankt Knuds Vej 11,
basement left, DK-1903 Frederiksberg, Denmark.
Tel.: +45 35 43 60 40, Fax: +45 35 43 87 57. e-mail:
eirdk@hotmail.com.

Mexico City: EIR, Sor Juana Inés de la Cruz 242-2
Col. Agricultura C.P. 11360
Delegación M. Hidalgo, México D.F.
Tel. (5525) 5318-2301
eirmexico@gmail.com

Canada Post Publication Sales Agreement
#40683579

Postmaster: Send all address changes to *EIR*, P.O.
Box 17390, Washington, D.C. 20041-0390.

Signed articles in *EIR* represent the views of the authors,
and not necessarily those of the Editorial Board.

Toward a Second Treaty of Westphalia

Trump Visit Launches New Era in U.S.-China Relations

by William Jones

Nov. 12—The three-day visit of President Donald Trump to the People's Republic of China for talks with Chinese President Xi Jinping has laid the basis for an entirely new type of relationship between the United States and China, and built the framework for cooperation for a policy of global development. Not since President Nixon went to China on his first historic visit 45 years ago, has a visit of a U.S. President to China had such profound implications for the world.

Before President Trump left on his 11-day trip to Asia, the media and the pundits were filled with articles claiming that the President was going to create a provocation against the DPRK (North Korea), give a dressing down to the South Korean President for being soft on the DPRK, and wrangle on trade issues with the Chinese President.

But none of that happened. On the contrary, in his encounters with Japanese Prime Minister Shinzo Abe, with South Korean President Moon Jae-in, and most decisively with Chinese President Xi Jinping, President Donald Trump proved himself an eminent statesman, leaving each leader with the clear feeling that this visit by the U.S. President had been a tremendous success.

While President Trump's task on his lengthy Asia tour was in part to reassure allies that the United States was not turning its back on this all-important region of the world, he did not come in as the belligerent leader of some threatening coalition, but rather as a friend and

White House/Andrea Hanks

President Xi (left) and President Trump being greeted Nov. 10 during his visit to China.

collaborator with each leader. While he minced no words in speaking to the South Korean National Assembly about his disdain for the policies of the North Korean leadership, at the same time he pointed out that there could be a "brighter path for North Korea," if it were willing to relinquish its nuclear ambitions. More important, he came to Asia with the understanding that the rising importance of China in the world community was not a threat but an opportunity—an opportunity to change the direction of politics, toward a more peaceful and prosperous world for all peoples.

What the media and the pundits also ignored in their ominous predictions, was the fact that the U.S. President had already established a substantial and close relationship with the Chinese President, as a result of their four personal meetings and numerous phone calls and messages. President Trump had sent congratulations to President Xi after the 19th Party Congress accepted Xi's new direction in policy with his proposal for a "new era" in China's foreign policy, and had incorporated the goals of President Xi's seminal Belt and Road Initiative into the Communist Party's constitution. And President Trump's unusual invitation earlier this year to President Xi and his wife to visit him at his home in Mar-a-Lago, provided an extraordinary personal touch, the significance of which did not go unnoticed by the Chinese leader.

More Than a State Visit

And the Chinese President more than reciprocated this kindness in the welcome he gave to President Trump and his wife, Melania, in Beijing. It was labeled a "state visit-plus" by the Chinese Ambassador to the United States, Cui Tiankai, and a "state visit-plus-plus" by President Xi! Neither level of welcome has ever occurred before.

In an extraordinary gesture, the historic Forbidden City, previously the home of the Chinese emperors, was entirely closed, and it was prepared as the venue for a private dinner with a foreign dignitary Nov. 8. While many major foreign guests, and in particular heads of state, often visit the Forbidden City when they first come to Beijing, this was the first time since the founding of the People's Republic of China in 1949 that a foreign dignitary was invited to dine in a palace of the Forbidden City. The President and his wife were also treated to three performances of Peking Opera plays at the Belvedere of Pleasant Sounds, the largest opera theater in the Forbidden City, initially built during the reign of Emperor Qianlong (1736-1795) in the Qing Dynasty to entertain the members of the imperial family. The three performances they viewed were *Spring Seedlings in the Pear Garden*, *The Drunken Concubine*, and the ever-popular *The Monkey King*, who in the famous Ming novel accompanied the monk Xuanzang on his epic journey to the West. President Trump posted a picture of the two Presidential couples with the Chinese actors, as the main banner on his Twitter account!

Xinhua/Rao Aimin

First Lady and President Trump being welcomed by China President Xi Jinping (center) and his wife, Peng Liyuan (right) at the square outside the East Gate of of the Great Hall of the People in Beijing, Nov. 9, 2017.

And the guide for the President and his wife on a tour of the Palace Museum located in the Forbidden City, was none other than President Xi himself. Both President Xi and his wife, Peng Liyuan, took President Trump and his wife, Melania, on a tour through the Forbidden City. And what better guide for such a tour than the Chinese President, whose keen sense of the history of the Chinese people is so much a fabric of his own being. More than a tour through a famous monument, this was undoubtedly an extremely important exposure for the U.S President to the long arc of Chinese history and culture—a culture which most profoundly shapes the attitudes and the policies of China today.

President Trump in turn showed President Xi and his wife a videotape of his 6-year old granddaughter, Arabella Kushner, who started learning Chinese when she was 18 months old. Arabella had already performed for President Xi and his wife when they visited President Trump in Mar-a-Lago in April, and has become quite a celebrity in China ever since. The couples viewed the video on an IPad while in the Forbidden City. Arabella greeted "Grandpa Xi" and "Grandma Peng" in Chinese, characterizing the closeness and respect exhibited by Trump family members toward the Chinese couple following the Mar-a-Lago visit. She then sang several songs and recited from a number of Chinese poems which she knew by heart—to the delight of her audience.

The next day, President Trump and the First lady arrived at the Great Hall of the People for President Trump's formal meetings with President Xi. He was greeted at the bottom of the steps by President Xi and Madame Peng, and was then escorted by the Chinese President to a reviewing stand outside the Great Hall where he reviewed military formations assembled there in his honor and received a 21-gun salute. The two presidents then individually greeted all the members of both delegations lined up before the Great Hall, before proceeding into the building for the formal discussions.

The major issues to be covered, and those most reported on in the media were: trade, the DPRK nuclear program, and the future development of U.S.-China relations. But they also touched on the Middle East, Afghanistan, counterterrorism, anti-drug cooperation, non-proliferation, and nuclear security. The two presidents committed to make the most of the four high-level dialogue mechanisms: the diplomatic and security dialogue, the comprehensive economic dialogue, the social and people-to-people dialogue, and the cyber-security dialogue, in order to achieve greater results in their cooperation.

In remarks to the press conference following their meeting, President Xi underlined the importance of the enhanced economic cooperation between the two countries. "It is necessary to formulate and launch an economic cooperation plan for the next phase to have continued in-depth discussion on trade imbalance, export, investment environment, market openness, and other issues, and work to support practical cooperation in energy, infrastructure, the Belt and Road Initiative, and other areas."

Following the meeting, the two presidents signed agreements and memoranda of understanding worth $250 billion. China agreed to purchase 300 aircraft from Boeing. China has also signed an agreement to purchase natural gas from Alaska. In this agreement between the State of Alaska and Alaska Gasline Development Corporation, on the one side, and Chinese Sinopec, China Investment Corporation, and the Bank of China, on the other, China will invest $43 billion, which is expected to create 12,000 new jobs in the U.S.A. There is also an $84 billion plan for China to invest in shale gas and chemical manufacturing projects in West Virginia. A memorandum of understanding was signed to that effect. Another deal involves China purchasing Liquified Natural Gas from Louisiana. All in all, over 37 major deals were signed, including deals by three companies heavily involved in the Belt and Road Initiative—Caterpillar, Honeywell, and General Electric—and Dow Chemical Company.

Partnership and Dialogue of Cultures

But far more important than the individual trade deals coming out of these negotiations, was the strengthening of the personal relationship between the leaders of two of the most important countries in the world. In his comments to the press following the meetings, President Trump underlined the real significance of the visit: "The United States, working with China and other regional partners, has an incredible opportunity to advance the cause of peace, security, and prosperity all across the world. It's a very special time, and we do indeed have that very, very special opportunity. A great responsibility has been placed on our shoulders, President—it's truly a great responsibility—and I hope we can rise to the occasion and help our countries and our citizens reach their highest destinies and their fullest potentials."

He then expressed his heartfelt appreciation for the warmth shown him by the Chinese President in the course of the visit. "I want to thank you again—you're a very special man—for your gracious hospitality. I send my warmest regards to your citizens. I honor their heritage and celebrate their great, great possibilities and potential for the future."

After the day's events, the President and his delegation were invited to a state banquet held in the Golden Hall Room in the Great Hall of the People. There they viewed scenes from the previous meetings of the two presidents at Mar-a-Lago and clips from President Trump's present visit to Beijing, and, to everyone's delight, were shown a big-screen version of the performance of Arabella Kushner.

In his comments at the banquet, President Xi himself compared Trump's visit to the visit of President Nixon 45 years ago, noting the tremendous importance of that visit in re-establishing U.S.-China relations: "President Trump, the state visit to China is another event of historic importance. Over the past two days, we have had in-depth exchange of views on how China and the United States should seize the opportunity, rise up to the challenges, and open up new grounds in our relations. Together, we have mapped out a blueprint for

White House

Presidents Trump and Xi Jinping at the APEC Summit, Nov. 11, 2017.

very deep respect for the heritage of your country and the noble traditions of its people. Your ancient values bring past and future together into the present. So beautiful! It is my hope that the proud spirits of the American and Chinese people will inspire our efforts to achieve a more just, secure, and peaceful world, a future worthy of the sacrifices of our ancestors, and the dreams of our children."

Re-read these comments of Presidents Trump and Xi. Ponder their significance! The implications of what we are witnessing are historic, and contain the potential to change the life of every person on this planet for the better. It is a potential for moving the entire world into an era of peace and economic development. Its significance goes far beyond the geo-political motives of Nixon's trip in 1972.

But true to form, the moronic voices of the U.S news media and political pundits have already been raised in "critiquing" President Trump's performance in China, carping about his "failure" to raise certain issues. All they are accomplishing in these complaints is revealing their own anti-Trump bias and their dismal failure to understand the fundamental forces that are now shaping history, because the world no longer operates under the banner of some world "hegemon."

The problems facing mankind are far too complex and difficult for any one country, be it China or the United States, to resolve. Only in a collaborative effort among all nations including the United States, China, and Russia, can poverty be eliminated, wars stopped or prevented, and world development promoted. The desperate attempts by the "Atlanticist" crowd to demonize the Russian President and to paint a diabolical picture of China's motives behind the ambitious Belt and Road Initiative, would only serve to make America irrelevant as the rest of the world comes together to forge a common destiny for mankind. President Trump wants to collaborate with China and with Russia in order to begin to tackle those world problems that can only be resolved through such collaboration. Should not every patriotic American give their support to this noble cause, and help re-establish that respect and honor in the eyes of the world community that this nation throughout its history has so long enjoyed—and deserved?

advancing China-U.S. relations. We both agree that China and the United States should remain partners, not rivals. We both agree that when we work together, we can accomplish many great things to the benefit of our two countries and the whole world."

In his comments, President Trump again emphasized his gratitude for the kindness and hospitality shown by his Chinese hosts, and stressed his understanding of the significance of the visit: "Yesterday, we visited the Forbidden City, which stands as a proud symbol of China's rich culture and majestic spirit. Your nation is a testament to thousands of years of vibrant, living history. And today, it was a tremendous honor to be greeted by the Chinese delegation right here at the Great Hall of the People. This moment in history presents both our nations with an incredible opportunity to advance peace and prosperity alongside other nations all around the world. In the words of a Chinese proverb, 'We must carry forward the cause and forge ahead into the future.' I am confident that we can realize this wonderful vision, a vision that will be so good and, in fact, so great for both China and the United States.

"Though we come from different places and faraway lands," Trump continued, "there is much that binds the East and West. Both of our countries were built by people of great courage, strong culture, and a desire to trek across the unknown into great danger. But they overcame. The people of the United States have a

EIR Contents

www.larouchepub.com Volume 44, Number 46, November 17, 2017

Xinhua/Lan Hongguang

Stopping Bob Mueller's Coup: Where We Stand

by Barbara Boyd

Nov. 13—It has been a little over six weeks since *EIR* first published the dossier, "Robert Mueller Is An Amoral Legal Assassin: He Will Do His Job If You Let Him." Our aim was to bring an end to the coup which has paralyzed the government of the United States, to the detriment of its suffering citizens, and to cause the investigation and prosecution of its perpetrators. When we started this campaign, Robert Mueller was considered the paragon of the highest knightly virtue the Washington swamp and national news media are wont to recognize among their tribe. You know, this is the PR babble crafted by those who have already sold their souls, and are in an incessant subconscious process of examining plausible virtues they once possessed, all in preparation for that righteous moment when they arrive at St. Peter's Gate.

Now, exposed by us and other brave souls, Strait-Laced Bobby Three Sticks, our homegrown Torquemada, and his merry band of torturers and assassins, are engaged in a mad race against time. The very grounds for the investigation itself keep blowing up as more and more truth is pulled from the kicking and screaming participants in the conspiracy against the President. Torquemada II, et al., are racing to secure scalps as the very grounds for their investigation begin to crater all around them. Reviewing the situation, such voices as the *Wall Street Journal* have called for Mueller's resignation and investigations of the FBI, calls which are now echoed on the floor and in the halls of Congress, and in serious subpoenas aimed at the coupmeisters.

Equally important, Mueller et al., have begun to be

Xinhua

Robert Mueller leaving Senate hearings, June 2017.

ridiculed and mocked. Humor and irony, the most devastating weapon against all overly pretentious tyrants, finally showed up in this fight, in the form of David Stockman's very well placed takedown of Mueller's indictment of Baby George Papadopoulos. "*This is how the Deep State crushes disobedience by the unwashed American public,*" Stockman begins. "It indicts not only ham sandwiches but, apparently, political infants in diapers too, if that's what it takes. Hence the sudden notoriety of Baby George Papadopoulos, who pled guilty to 'lying' about an essentially immaterial date to the FBI."

But, we are only part of the way on our journey. The republic remains in peril. On Saturday, November 11, the President rightly called out Obama's intelligence chiefs as political hacks, and said that the Mueller investigation was an outright fraud. That

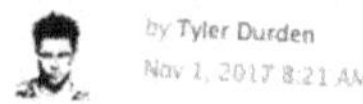

David Stockman exposed Robert Mueller in this Nov. 1 posting on the ZeroHedge website.

should have been greeted with calls for Mueller's resignation by the Congress and by other national leaders. There should have been editorials to the same effect from every newspaper in the land. An aroused citizenry should be forming pitchfork brigades focused, like lasers, on defending our Constitution, and not allowing an unhinged and illegitimate prosecutor to take out the sitting President of this great nation.

We are calling on you to help us finish this job. If you haven't read the Mueller dossier yet, you can read it here. This progress report only relates as much of that document as is essential to explain the developments since it was published.

Get active. Tell your Congressmen, tell any other public official responsive to you, tell your union chief, and tell your neighbors and friends, that the Mueller Special Counsel farce must end, and that you will not take "no" for an answer. That kind of focus sets the right public climate for full exposure of those involved in the coup against the President, and for prosecution of their crimes. John Brennan, James Clapper, James Comey, Barack Obama, and Hillary Clinton are not just political hacks. They used the official powers of the United States, in full collusion with the British Secret Services, to first attack an American presidential campaign and then launch an insurrection against the elected President. These are crimes which cannot go unpunished.

Motives for the Coup Remain the Same

We wrote the dossier looking ahead to President Trump's visit to China, which seemed imperiled by the momentum of the coup. As we outlined in depth there, the motive for the coup against the President has nothing to do with any of the arguments advanced by the nation's offended, Trump-deranged, and bankrupt elites. Behind closed doors, the Party of Davos is white with fear over the huge economic development projects now proceeding in the world under the auspices of China. This new paradigm for international relations is already substantively transforming economic relations in the world, and leaving the bankrupt Anglo-American imperial elites to stew in their mountain of unpayable debt. Their system collapsed in 2008 and never recovered, and now the same tired Wall Street recipes that led to the collapse have resulted in a speculative bubble even larger than 2008.

Trump really likes China's President Xi Jinping, but not because he is a ruthless dictator and all authoritarians love one another, as posited by our lame-brained "elites." As opposed to the sophomoric elite analysis, Trump likes Xi because Xi has a compelling vision of the future in which poverty is eliminated in this world, and mankind happily functions on the highest plane of scientific and technological progress. The same people who have criminally attacked this President, are engaged in suppressing the real news about what China is doing, and what Trump wants to do in collaboration with them.

With respect to Russia—Barack Obama and Hillary Clinton, egged on by the British, began a new Cold War with Russia in 2014 when they staged a neo-Nazi coup in Ukraine, overthrowing Ukrainian President Victor Yanukovych, as a stepping stone in their ultimate plan for regime change in Russia itself. President Trump rejected the Putin regime-change operation—a sure path to World War III—and continues to insist that the

Presidents Donald Trump and Vladimir Putin shake hands at the APEC Summit in Da Nang, Vietnam.

world's two most heavily nuclear armed powers must find a way to get along.

On November 11, the President spoke again to President Putin at the APEC summit about the allegation of Russian election meddling. Putin again denied it. The President went on to tell the press on his plane afterwards, that Mueller's investigation is a farce which could cost thousands of human lives, as it impedes his ability to resolve the Korean crisis and the conflicts in Ukraine and Syria by engaging with Russia. He declared it a Democratic hit job engineered by political hacks in Obama's intelligence community, including Comey, Brennan, and Clapper. The entire establishment instantly responded with collective shrieks and solemn denunciations of the President for misbehaving yet again. Based on the evidence now available, the President's condemnation of Obama's political hacks, masquerading as intelligence chiefs, was a mild statement of the case.

Sane Voices in Congress

As we wrote in our Mueller dossier, there are two central propositions in the ongoing coup against the President: (1) Russians hacked the computers of the Democratic National Committee and John Podesta; WikiLeaks published the Russian-hacked emails showing that Hillary Clinton and the DNC were rigging the Democratic Party primary against Bernie Sanders; and (2) Russia had an ongoing relationship with Donald Trump, had compromised him, and worked through social media and other means to secure his election.

Both of these claims originate with British intelligence. According to British media reports, the British began pounding their American intelligence counterparts in 2015 with claims about Trump's Russian associations and about Russian hacking of the DNC computers. These claims were formalized, beginning in June 2016, in a dossier put together by "former" MI6 agent Christopher Steele, which Steele says he first passed to the FBI in July 2016. Steele's work was contracted by the U.S. political smear firm, Fusion GPS, which has had a longstanding relationship with Steele and his British intelligence colleagues dating from 2010. In July 2016, when the dossier was passed to James Comey's FBI, it began an unprecedented counterintelligence investigation of an American presidential campaign, seeking to corroborate what have proven to be fake and fabricated British claims about Trump.

In September 2016, according to his sworn declaration in a London Court, Christopher Steele came to the United States and briefed Michael Isikoff of Yahoo News, and reporters for the *New York Times*, the *Washington Post*, CNN, and the *New Yorker* on his "research." He conducted further briefings with the same reporters for the *New York Times*, *Washington Post*, and Isikoff in October, adding *Mother Jones* reporter David Corn to his briefing tree. Comey's FBI investigation otherwise leaked widely to the press. The claims made in the Steele dossier, however, just did not check out, and except for shorter pieces by Isikoff and David Corn, reporters avoided Steele's most salacious false allegations rather than risk libel suits. But, between Comey's FBI investigation, the press rumor mill, and public letters to the FBI by Senator Harry Reid, enough smoke was created to allow the Clinton campaign and Barack Obama to charge Donald Trump with being Putin's Manchurian Candidate throughout the final two months of the presidential campaign. They cited anonymous U.S. government sources to frame what was in their

CSPAN

Congressman Adam Schiff.

minds a public charge of treason against the Republican presidential nominee.

Ever since the beginning of the Russiagate investigation in Congress, the Intelligence and the Judiciary committees of both houses have sought to find out who paid for Christopher Steele's Dossier, and how it was used by Obama's intelligence agencies and the FBI. Steele had a longstanding relationship with the FBI, including, many believe, with Assistant Director Andrew McCabe, and the FBI offered to pay Steele to continue his "project" after the election.

The Congressional committees were effectively stonewalled by Fusion GPS and the FBI—stonewalling fully abetted by Hollywood's watermelon-headed Congressman, Adam Schiff, who played Robespierre within the House Intelligence Committee itself, while orchestrating a steady round of media defamations against House Intelligence Committee Chairman Devin Nunes. Only in early October 2017 did sane voices finally prevail in the House Intelligence Committee. A subpoena was issued for Fusion's bank records, generating an intense fight in the United States District Court for the District of Columbia, in which Schiff and Fusion continued their juvenile tirades against Devin Nunes. The Court was not impressed.

The Facade Crumbles: New Crimes Revealed

On October 24, the law firm Perkins, Coie released a letter as part of settlement negotiations in that court case, containing the stunning revelation that Hillary Clinton's campaign itself paid for the Steele dossier along with the Clinton-controlled Democratic National Committee. The payments were laundered through Perkins, Coie, which was general counsel for both the Clinton campaign and the DNC. Perkins, Coie has otherwise long been associated with Barack Obama. The payments were never specifically reported to the FEC, despite their clear and intentional impact on the election and a clear legal requirement to report them. Rather, they were lumped into the general category of "legal expenses."

So now you know. The Clinton campaign and the DNC paid a British spy to produce trash for cash on Donald Trump, and deliberately disguised this foreign intervention into the American presidential campaign and the payments for it. It is a fabricated smear job; the equivalent of a British tabloid hit-piece written by someone at a high level in Her Majesty's Secret Services. The FBI legitimized this cash-for-trash product, paid for by Donald Trump's political opponent, by using it to initiate surveillance of the Trump campaign under E.O. 12333 and, in all probability, through warrants granted by the FISA Court, probably as the result of omissions and false statements by the Justice Department and the FBI.

The very "caught" Hillary Clinton and her surrogates are now making the rounds trying to minimize it all, lying their heads off by saying that the Steele dossier was not that important and had no impact on the election because it only "came out" after the election.

While the Fusion GPS bank subpoena was being fought out in Court, House Speaker Paul Ryan personally intervened with the Department of Justice, demanding the FBI's files concerning its use of the Steele dossier. Within the past days, those files were viewed for the first time by staff of the House Intelligence Committee. The House had subpoenaed the FBI for these documents in September, but the subpoena was simply ignored by the FBI.

As of this writing, the House Intelligence Committee is back in Court, seeking more bank records from Fusion concerning payments to journalists to push the Steele dossier. In addition, the House Intelligence and Senate Judiciary committees are seeking all applications for FISA warrants in the FBI's Russiagate and related investigations, to determine whether Steele's discredited and unverified claims were used in these proceedings. The two committees are also seeking to find out why the FBI offered to pay Steele to continue his "investigations" after the election, an offer made in full knowledge that his original claims didn't check out, that he had paid his so-called Russian informants, and that his work constituted a political hit job for the Clinton presidential campaign.

Meanwhile, the role of Barack Obama, Susan Rice, Samantha Power, and Obama's intelligence chiefs, in unlawfully using official government surveillance and investigative powers first to campaign against Trump, and then to undermine him, remains very much a hot Washington topic. Ed Klein, for example, recently alleged that Valerie Jarrett was up to her ears in coordinating actions against Trump directly from the Obama White House on behalf of the President.

Now think about all of this in the context of the infamous intelligence briefing of Trump in January 2017 by Obama officials. That is the briefing in which Clapper, Brennan, et al. stepped aside, leaving James Comey alone to brief the incoming President on the Steele dossier. Comey himself called this a "J. Edgar Hoover moment" in Senate testimony. There was only one—extortive—purpose behind the event: Change your idea on Putin, and we'll keep the salacious sexual allegations regarding you and Russian prostitutes in the Steele dossier from public view. Trump instead denounced the Steele memo as a fraud, and demanded that Comey investigate and debunk it. Brennan, Clapper, and Comey immediately ginned up its widespread publication, giving the Clinton campaign's illicit garbage the imprimatur of grave and official seriousness. Political hacks? The President was absolutely correct.

White House/Pete Souza

President Obama listens to Valerie Jarrett during a senior staff meeting in the Oval Office, August 13, 2009.

June Meeting Stinks Worse Than Ever

Soon after Steele's discredited allegations began to circulate in intelligence circles during Spring 2016, the race was on to infiltrate the Trump campaign and set it up, to entrap it. It is extremely likely that such infiltration attempts, from the British side, even preceded the circulation of the dossier. Anyone familiar with U.S. counterintelligence operations under E.O. 12333 knows that is what had to happen.

In our Mueller dossier we go into great detail about the June 2016 meeting at Trump Tower between Donald Trump, Jr., Paul Manafort, Jared Kushner, and Russian lawyer Natalia Veselnitskaya. We lay out the number of intelligence agencies that were provably involved in the setup for this meeting, and the very strange State Department visa allowing Veselnitskaya to even enter the United States for the meeting. This meeting has been a central event in Mueller's investigation, including most recently whether President Trump was involved in making "false exculpatory statements" when he helped his son, Donald Jr., craft an initial statement about the meeting. That's right folks—we're in the world of complete prosecutorial overreach and craziness here. In Mueller's world, you're not allowed to defend yourself; only the prosecutor's version of events is allowed.

In recent coverage, the *New York Times* et al., working off leaks from Mueller, have been frothing over the claim that the talking points that Veselnitskaya brought to the meeting about the Magnitsky Act, the Ziff Brothers, and the Clinton campaign, had been previously submitted by Veselnitskaya to Russia's Prosecutor General, Yury Chaika.

We have just learned however, that Veselnitskaya's talking points for the meeting did not even originate in

Russia. Rather, they were written by Fusion GPS, Christopher Steele's nominal U.S. employer—the same firm that was under a million dollar contract to Hillary Clinton and the Democratic National Committee for purposes of destroying Donald Trump. Fusion, at the time, was also under contract to Veselnitskaya's Russian clients in a lawsuit in the Southern District of New York. It should be obvious now that the setup for this meeting should be the topic of criminal investigation. The Trump campaign was the victim of an extraordinary intelligence community entrapment attempt, facilitated with funds from a political opponent.

William Binney at an event hosted by EIR *in New York, Sept. 9, 2017.*

Binney Gets a Hearing, Washington Goes Nuts

Now let's return for a moment to the first premise of the coup, to wit, that the Russians hacked the DNC's server and John Podesta's email account, revealing that the DNC was rigging the primary elections on behalf of Hillary Clinton. On June 12, WikiLeaks announced that it was in possession of emails damaging to Clinton and would soon release them. On June 14, the DNC publicly announced that its computers had been hacked by the Russians. This claim is in the second memo of Christopher Steele's dossier, and the British, by their own account, had been telling the FBI that the DNC computers had been hacked since 2015. The FBI says it passed this warning to the DNC. The DNC, according to even the official narrative, sat on this information until two days after WikiLeaks announced that it had the goods on Hillary Clinton. WikiLeaks, of course, also had a treasure trove of

Dmitri Alperovitch, co-founder of CrowdStrike, speaking at the World Economic Forum, Jan. 22, 2016.

Clinton's State Department emails that had previously been publicized. According to the official narrative, the Russians, through WikiLeaks, meddled by using the hacked emails to damage Clinton's candidacy, by proving what was already evident to any sentient observer, that the Democratic presidential primaries were rigged for Hillary Clinton.

As if this adventure in Wonderland were not enough, the DNC never turned its allegedly hacked computers over to the FBI for analysis. Rather, attorneys for Perkins, Coie—that's right, the same firm pimping the Steele dossier—hired CrowdStrike, a computer security firm. CrowdStrike is headed by the violently anti-Russian Dmitri Alperovitch of the Atlantic Council, and also features Shawn Harvey, formerly of Robert Mueller's FBI cyber-security unit.

The Atlantic Council, in collaboration with MI6 and NATO, has, since 2014, produced most of the claptrap about Russian social media posts and bots kidnapping the Western mind through persuasive messages—the stuff which is the anti-Russia hysteria *du jour* at present in the U.S. Congress. The Council is funded by Britain's Foreign and Commonwealth Office, Abu Dhabi's national oil company, the Ukrainian World Congress, the U.S. State Department, Raytheon, Lockheed, and the Ukrainian oligarch Victor Pinchuk.

Shawn Harvey, while at the FBI, presided over a contingent of computer hackers adept at counterintelligence operations against nation states deemed hostile to the United States, and of criminal hackers who had been compromised by the FBI. (Some analysts familiar with this history have recently pointed to Alperovitch and Harvey as the possible creators of the persona known as Guccifer 2.0.)

CrowdStrike predictably pronounced that Russia was the culprit in the hacking of the DNC, and James Comey's FBI accepted this analysis without so much as a second look.

William Binney, the former technical director of the NSA, has consistently noted that the NSA was in a position to prove the source of any hack of the DNC, down to the location of the alleged hackers. He knows because he is intimately familiar with NSA systems he helped design that can track any Internet traffic anywhere in the world. The NSA has never come forward with that information or any other evidence for the Russian hack, despite the claims by Senators and intelligence chiefs that the Russian hacking amounted to an "act of war." Moreover, Binney is a key signator of the July 24, 2017 Veteran Intelligence Professionals for Sanity (VIPS) "Memo to the President," demonstrating that there was no Russian hack of the DNC as claimed. Rather, the WikiLeaks documents were the probable product of a leak from inside the DNC, not a hack.

The VIPS report points out that the CIA's "Marble Framework" program enables the user to carry out a cyberattack while obfuscating its source, and to create false-flag attribution of the attack to another state actor.

On October 24, Bill Binney met with CIA Director Mike Pompeo at the specific request of President Trump. According to Binney's account, Pompeo asked him whether he would be willing to discuss his findings with the FBI or other investigators, and Binney pledged his cooperation. The reaction in official Washington was apoplectic. First Binney was painted as a "conspiracy theorist" and a "Russia hack denier" by the main stream media. Pompeo was denounced for no longer being a "neutral" arbiter between the President of the United States and the CIA, as if that were an appropriate and Constitutional job description.

Then, the *New York Times* announced that the FBI and Justice Department were prepared to indict six Russians for the DNC and Podesta hacks, sometime in 2018. Next, Mueller's office leaked that it was looking at a September meeting between Congressmen Dana Rohrabacher and Michael Flynn as part of its inquisition against Trump. Rohrabacher has been trying to

CSPAN

Andrew Weissman

broker a deal with Julian Assange of WikiLeaks, involving production of Assange's proof that the Russians did not hack the DNC and that WikiLeaks was rather the recipient of an inside leak. As I said, official Washington is apoplectic on this point—don't listen, don't listen, don't listen to Binney—he could really blow it all up.

In its story on the putative 2018 Russian indictments for the DNC hack, the *New York Times* also, casually, referenced a real shocker. The *Times* wrote that Mueller is not investigating the DNC or Podesta hacks. It says he left that to the FBI as the result of some bureaucratic decision about a division of labor. But, isn't that what Mueller is supposed to be investigating under his DOJ mandate? Instead we have Manafort's dealings in Ukraine, and Flynn's dealings with Turkey. Does the very heavy-handed hysteria over Binney, along with Mueller's avoidance of a central element of his mandate, tell us that the investigation of this issue—the non-existent DNC and Podesta hacks—is the axe that could bring down all the trees in this rotting and malodorous forest?

About Those Indictments

In our Mueller dossier, we laid out Mueller's history as an amoral political hit-man, starting with the case of Lyndon LaRouche and proceeding through the intentional coverup of the Saudi role in 9/11—conducted while he played a major role in constructing our post-9/11 police state. He has left a trail of victims whose lives he has destroyed through torture (his post-9/11 roundup and torture of Muslims) and outright persecution of the innocent (Steven Hatfill and others). Mueller's FBI became an entrapment machine under the guise of combatting terrorism, with a national informant "Linked In" type of switchboard, allowing agents to dial up the compromised individual of their choice.

Mueller's prosecutorial team is led by Andrew Weissman, a veteran of his Enron prosecution whom he has mentored throughout Weissman's career. The Enron prosecution illegally destroyed the Arthur Andersen accounting firm and numerous innocent individuals who simply did business with Enron. The Supreme Court and the lower federal courts in those cases strongly rebuked Weissman and other Enron prosecutors for inventing crimes that did exist, a stinging rebuke that in former times would have ended their legal careers. (See Sidney Powell, *Licensed to Lie: Exposing Corruption in the Department of Justice*. Houston: Brown Books Publishing Group, 2014.)

Law professor Alan Dershowitz has made the very valid point that with this special prosecutor, and other recent investigations, we have entered the dangerous realm of prosecuting thought, of criminalizing political differences. As we outlined in our Mueller dossier, the LaRouche prosecution was a full-blown manifestation of that evil legal development. Thought crimes, the criminalization of political differences, otherwise characterize the theory of law popularized by the Nazi Crown Jurist Carl Schmitt. The establishment violently disagrees with Trump's view of Putin and Russia. It has enlisted the media and various compromised and deluded Congressmen to demonize both Trump and Putin around the clock. Mueller and his legal inventions are the chosen means to enforce the establishment's view.

If anyone should doubt our perspective, the Paul Manafort indictment—recently delivered by Mueller— is a case study. First and foremost, the indictment has nothing to do with the 2016 Presidential campaign or Putin's alleged collusion with Trump, although the Steele dossier names Manafort as the manager of the electoral collusion between Russia and Trump.

Rather, Paul Manafort's actual sin was assisting Ukraine's Yanukovych and his Party of the Regions in Ukrainian electoral efforts. He chose the wrong side in opposing Obama's and Clinton's 2014 neo-Nazi Ukrainian coup, and got paid, apparently handsomely, for making that choice. Manafort's Ukrainian activities are the gravamen of Mueller's charges against him. It is

Paul Manafort, turning himself in to the FBI, October 2017.

unclear at this point how much of the information for Mueller's charges against Manafort is the result of the same Hillary Clinton/DNC foreign operations implicated in the Steele dossier. The Clinton campaign openly collaborated with Ukrainian state intelligence when it first surfaced the charges against Paul Manafort's financial dealings in Ukraine. The Clinton charges resulted in Manafort's resignation from the Trump campaign right after the Republican Convention.

In unsealing the indictment, Mueller claimed, histrionically, that Manafort was charged with "CONSPIRACY AGAINST THE UNITED STATES," in capital letters. This is not actually even a real criminal charge. The conspiracy has to be a conspiracy to do something, such as a conspiracy to defraud. But Mueller was looking for headlines consistent with the "Red Under Every Bed" and "Red Behind Every Facebook Friend Request" fever presently infecting official Washington and the mainstream media. In reality, Manafort is charged in multiple counts with a conspiracy to avoid registering under the Foreign Agents Registration Act, false statements associated with his Foreign Agents Registration Act statement, and failure to file the Treasury Department forms required by the Bank Secrecy Act. The indictment abusively features multiple charges for essentially the same act, and is sure to be challenged on double-jeopardy grounds.

While it can be a crime not to register under the Foreign Agents Registration Act (FARA), the Justice Department rarely prosecutes such cases, having brought only seven cases in 40 years. Rather, the Justice Department's practice is to encourage registration, and the DOJ regularly allows retroactive registration without criminal charges. This facilitates the major industry of our nation's capital—lobbying Congress for huge sums of money.

Against this background it is not a stretch to call this prosecution selective and vindictive. If Manafort is getting creamed because of lobbying and not filling out the right forms for a political party in Ukraine, and making obscene amounts of money for it—what about the well-established and more powerful lobbies for Israel, Saudi Arabia, and others? Mueller et al. are apparently conscious enough of this problem to have opened full blown investigations against the other lobbyists involved with Ukraine's Party of the Regions, Tony Podesta (John Podesta's brother), and former Congressman Vin Weber. As of this writing, Tony Podesta's lobbying firm is on the verge of collapse because of Mueller's investigation.

Go After the Defense Lawyers

And for final measure in this case, the Mueller team has already begun to go after the lawyers defending his targets, as is Mueller's historic practice. In a profession with more than its share of those who "go along to get along," aggressive defense tactics are truly tempered when jail for the lawyer is put on the table.

The Judge in charge of the District of Columbia U.S. District Court Grand Jury that indicted Manafort is Beryl A. Howell, the former Senate Judiciary Committee counsel for the hyper-partisan Senator Patrick Leahy. Howell is also a veteran of the same Eastern District of New York U.S. Attorney's office that produced Loretta Lynch and Andrew Weissman. Weissman and Howell have worked together before. In the Manafort Grand Jury, Weissman moved to force the testimony of one of the attorneys involved in the FARA filings by Manafort and co-defendant Rick Gates, voiding attorney-client privilege under the so-called crime fraud exception to that privilege. Howell merrily concurred and the lawyer was compelled to testify against her client.

The idea, in both the Manafort and soon-to-be-announced Michael Flynn indictments, is to force cooperation by piling up charges and possible jail sentences, not only against targets, but against their family members as well. In Michael Flynn's case it is an obvious attempt by put some meat onto James Comey's bogus charges of obstruction of justice by the President.

In the original scenario, Comey testified that Trump was seeking to obstruct justice by asking him to let the "Flynn matter" go, on the day Flynn was fired as National Security Advisor for lying to Vice-President Mike Pence. It is clear from the record that the "Flynn matter," at the time when Comey and the President spoke, involved possible false statements made by Flynn, without the benefit of counsel, to an FBI agent who interviewed Flynn about his interactions with the Russian Ambassador during the presidential transition. Hardly sexy in the realm of political prosecutions. Now Mueller and his press hacks are ginning up the "Flynn matter" to include a sensational and improbable plot to kidnap Turkish exile Fethullah Gülen and return him to Turkey for prosecution, with big bucks being paid to Flynn for the service rendered. Of course, the primary allegation against Flynn also involves novel uses of the Foreign Agents Registration Act.

Back to Russiagate and Baby George

Since the Manafort indictment clearly had nothing to do with the 2016 election, other than the opportunity to coerce false testimony against the President under threat of years in jail, Mueller took the opportunity, on the day that Manafort's indictment was unsealed, to also unseal a plea agreement from one George Papadopoulos, or Baby George, as caricatured accurately by David Stockman.

Stockman recounts how a 28-year-old know-nothing, who listed his college participation in a student role-playing exercise as a foreign policy credential on his "Linked In" page, came to be seated on the hastily created Trump Foreign Policy Advisory Council. Stockman says that Trump's twin perspectives of reaching an accommodation with Russia and obtaining his foreign policy views from watching TV, had deeply offended and enraged the Washington, D.C. foreign policy consensus. They kept pressing and pressing Trump to come up with names for his foreign policy team—which they were all collectively and publicly boycotting.

On March 21, 2016 Trump "announced a group of five advisors that exactly no one who was anyone in Imperial City had ever heard of and for good reason: The group included two recycled DOD flunkies, an anti-Muslim fanatic from the Lebanon religious wars, and two kids of no accomplishment in the foreign policy field whatsoever." With respect to Papadopoulos, *Politico* and the *Washington Post* pounced: the "kid had no more qualifications … than anyone else in the D.C. phone book—although at the time Baby George was called to duty, he was apparently domiciled in London and perhaps listed in their phone book." In the past 48 hours, however, with Mueller's imprimatur, Baby George has been turned into a master spy by the same publications.

"In a word, Baby George's 'crime' came about in the process of trying to put on his Big Boy Pants and get noticed by higher-ups in the campaign. So doing, he came into contact on about March 13 with a London professor who claimed to be plugged into Russian sources with 'dirt' about Hillary."

Needless to say, the London professor—one Joseph Mifsud, a Maltese whose sole foreign policy position had been as an assistant to the Maltese Foreign Minister—"didn't know anyone in the Kremlin either.... As it turned out, George never made any contact with Russian state officials, didn't have any meetings with clandestine Putin operatives, and came up with no anti-Hillary dirt at all—despite months of trying and sending loads of essentially unanswered emails up the chain of command at Trump Tower.... So, finding no contacts, no meetings, no 'collusion' or anything else validly related to Mueller's mandate, the latter's legal gunslingers came up with the usual default 'crime' ... To wit, Papadopoulos allegedly *perjured* himself by telling the FBI ... that he had met the no-count London professor *before* beginning his service as a Trump advisor." (He was off by a week, more or less, according to his plea bargain.)

Stockman concludes, "Anyone not involved in the campaign to reverse the 2016 election and remove the Donald from office should be forgiven for splitting a gut laughing when reading this hideous and utterly bogus case against Baby George Papadopoulos."

But Who Is Baby George?

While Stockman provides the right state of mind for examining this farce, it does not end there. Papadopoulos has the current classic profile of an intelligence community informant—the question is whether he is British or American, a shared asset, or simply a pliable dupe. His known means of financial support are extremely sketchy. His chief credential was his claimed years of work for the Hudson Institute. But he was not employed there. He was either an unpaid intern or a contracted research associate. He came to the Trump campaign after he worked for the Ben Carson campaign, where he applied via a "Linked In" application and was hired out of a similar desperation for someone with a foreign policy background. It turns out he was largely a no-show for the Carson campaign job, being paid to live in Washington, but moving to Chicago instead, to live with a girlfriend.

His ties to London are extensive. He got a master's degree in Security Studies at the University of London, worked for a London company, Energy Stream, and then made connections with London think-tanks associated with the weird Maltese Professor Mifsud.

Papadopoulos is a friend of Sergei Millian, the American of Belarus ancestry who formerly headed the Russian-American Business Association. Millian is an equally blank-backgrounded hustler who, according to various leaked media accounts, was Christopher Steele's "indirect" source for the most salacious allegations in Steele's dirty dossier against Trump. As with much of Steele's dossier, Millian himself is not the source of the allegations; rather he repeated them to Steele's actual source, described as a friend of Millian.

All the press accounts concerning Baby George, his friend Millian, and the mysterious Maltese professor are in almost identical formats. They have bragged repeatedly of connections between Russia and Trump, claiming an insider's knowledge of such connections, while most of their claims have proved outright false or exaggerated. All are described as ambitious hustlers who talk a load of bull. One can't help thinking about the FBI's dial-an-informant service.

Insist: This Must End!

Yes, the coup has been weakened since we produced the Mueller dossier six weeks ago. But Mueller's actions, detailed here, are the result of both his sordid history and his current imperative to protect and cover up the activities of the British, of Obama and Clinton, and of the Obama intelligence chiefs who now stand increasingly exposed. Mueller can only do that by fulfilling his charge to take out the President of the United States. If the country is to survive, Donald Trump cannot be put in further legal peril. The citizens have to cause Mueller's firing or retirement. The citizens have to pull Mueller's popular mandate. Call your Congressman. Call your state or local official. Call your other constituency leaders. Insist: This must end. The crimes involved in the coup against the President are what should be investigated and prosecuted. This nation's entire future is at stake. It really is time to bring down the curtain on this charade.

Beethoven's Fifth Symphony and Bernhard Riemann: How Minds Think

by David Shavin

China has put on the table the beautiful—and very "American"—mission of wiping out poverty by the year 2020. The type of thinking required today to finally wipe out poverty, disease and hunger will involve a level of creativity once described by Lyndon LaRouche as being able to "play ping-pong with the stars."

The beautiful composition of a new alliance of nations—pushing the frontiers of plasma physics, fusion technologies, and materials processing, as the surplus is deployed to craft massive infrastructure projects throughout the developing world—requires a level of thinking and emotional development that will make future generations stand in awe. This type of thinking is that of the "poet-mathematician." It was also expressed in Plato's Republic *as that of the "philosopher-king"—the almost impossible, but completely necessary development of leaders, who pursue the most difficult paradoxes in astronomy and music, so as to harmonize their souls with the complexities of the development of human communities.*

After the American Revolution, a youthful genius, Karl Gauss, in what was apparently an obscure mathematical text, went boldly where most others feared to tread. An identifiable, small core of youth, took up Gauss's challenge while he was alive. They were Sophie Germain, Lejeune Dirichlet, Niels Abel, Evariste

Ludwig van Beethoven (1770-1827)

Galois and Bernhard Riemann.

Nov. 12—This third article continues with the story of another of the primary students of Gauss's *Disquisitiones Arithmeticae*, Bernhard Riemann.

In Part I, we investigated the powerful inversion method of Niels Abel and the role of August Crelle's music salon in Abel's development.

In Part II, we found the dissymmetries of the Platonic dodecahedron to be central for Evariste Galois' genius—a subject championed by Edgar Allan Poe, with the invention of his unique thinker, C. Auguste Dupin.

In both cases, the singing quality behind what is considered "rigor" in mathematics, and the rigorous causality communicated in the free exercise of classical musical compositions, found a rich interplay. Now, we dig deeper into this subject, with Beethoven's bold scientific treatise, his Fifth Symphony, and its proper scientific development in Riemann's treatment of the subservience of measure-relations to a broader, topological character.

To begin, consider, if you will, an exhilarating and gripping musical theme. It is sixteen notes long ... and, by the way, the first twelve notes are all the same note.

How is that possible? The answer involves a re-evaluation of how you hear, how you talk, and how your mind is operating.

I. Beethoven's Unique Transformation

The most famous four notes in classical music, completely taken for granted by almost everyone, make up the signature of Beethoven's Fifth Symphony—the three short 1/8-notes on G, followed by a sustained E♭. Indeed, there are three of one thing and one of another, and this we may identify as a proportionality, 3:1. But, as we shall hear, of even greater weight is that one "thing" has a short quality and the other "thing," long. The germ of an idea, of a certain shape suggested by "short-short-short, long," we may tag as the "prosodic" idea, "sss-l."

A third factor, the tonal motion, which goes, in C minor, from the fifth to the minor third, usually is given the primary status. While certainly not unimportant, it is actually subsidiary to the prosodic shape. But, for the record, do note that this shaped idea, sss-l, is then repeated a scale-step lower, on new tones, the F and D. Over the next fifty-five or so measures, a closely-related but different idea—the proportional, or metrical, idea of 3:1—is given full play. But then Beethoven shows how his mind works. The key relationship of the two, the prosodic and the metrical, or this interplay of

(a) the mind's power of causally acting upon a prosodic idea, a shape—actually a "gestalt"—with

(b) the mind's power of measuring and handling proportionalities,

breaks onto the scene. (Listen to http://www.youtube.com/watch?v=xmwHOhSYJI4, including measures 59-65, 00:49-00:55.)

First, the French horns "stretch out" (or "augment") the original prosodic idea. The two-measure sss-l becomes an eight-measure sss-l. Here, each "short" part goes from a quarter-measure to a full measure, while the "long" part goes from one measure to four. (The tonal expanse, compared to the opening idea, also undergoes a stretching.) The space carved out by the French horns' augmentation has prepared a surprisingly "new" idea:

the violins play (00:53-00:55) a four-measure phrase that is peculiarly phrased as "three and one"—but now the "three" is attached with the "long," not with the original three short notes, and the "one" is attached with the "short." Pedants may label this the "second theme," but that obscures the underlying connection. Rather, the ear and the mind are thrown off guard, and are thrilled that Beethoven has apparently pulled apart the prosodic and metrical aspects, and then re-attached them—sort of a grand "inversion," an "inversion" not of a few notes, but of two different powers of the mind.

This bears a bit closer inspection. Yes, it is also the case that we are now in the key of E♭, and it is also related to the opening idea as sort of a tonal inversion of the original. But, as Brahms would (and did) say, in a similar situation: "Any donkey can hear that." The tonal relations are not driving what Beethoven is getting at. Rather, of more importance here (and what donkeys indeed have trouble with), the eight quarter-notes of the so-called "second theme" played by the violins are phrased in two groups: first a group of six and then a group of two. Beethoven bows (groups) them that way. This is the same 3:1 proportionality. So, now the "3" goes with the "long" and the "1" goes with the "short." The phrasing actually violates nature—and wonderfully so! More than a few orchestras balk at this hurdle, and phrase, as if on automatic pilot, the first four notes against the next four notes.[1] Beethoven's phrasing is, indeed, unnatural by almost any measure; however, he is much more interested in inverting the prosodic and the metrical capacities of the mind! While neither one is seen, both are experienced as felt realities in Beethoven's transformation. And the mind says, "That Beethoven fellow is speaking my language. Play on!"

Beethoven's 'Habilitation Paper'

Beethoven crafted a means of displaying to the human mind, the higher capacity of that same human mind, both (a) to think in gestalts, and (b) to measure, to create proportionalities. This is not simply to have gestalts, and then also to be able to carry out scalar measurements; but rather to design the type of measuring process based upon the evaluation of the characteristic of the gestalt. Hence, Bernhard Riemann.

---

1. Most conductors will at least dutifully abide by Beethoven's given bowing, though to little conviction or purpose. They will simply fail to bring out Beethoven's phrase, by flinching on, or swallowing, the last two notes. Herbert van Karajan provides one useful example. See 00:44-00:47 https://www.youtube.com/watch?v=XipZen3zlC8

Prior to Riemann, Beethoven's subject was treated by Plato, in terms of the combined, but separable, "integrative" and "critical" capacities of the mind. Notably, Gottfried Leibniz addressed this in terms of the role of the characteristic in his "analysis situs" approach, whereby Plato's "integrative" and "critical" are developed as integration and differentiation. (What is called "calculus" is a secondary offshoot of Leibniz's much more general and extensive integration and differentiation method. However, reducing Leibniz's method is, indeed, the necessary first step to even attempt to create a "priority dispute" with Isaac Newton.) For Beethoven, and the others, man's capacity to carry out measure in and upon the world (to establish metrical relations) is different from, and premised upon, his ("gestalt") capacity, to take in to oneself the whole shape of the idea, or integral unity, of the problem that he faces. At its core, this is the human condition—to be a mortal singularity with the capacity to act upon the whole world and upon all time.

Riemann's treatment of metrical possibilities, as stemming from the topological characteristic, liberated human culture from the shackles of Euclidean formalism. This is not simply to adopt "alternative-reality," non-Euclidean geometries, leaving the underlying hypotheses governing the new geometries still in control, and the mind still shackled. Riemann's very general and very powerful method developed a new language for the human species, to better mine the wealth of the powers of the mind.

II. Did Riemann Study Beethoven's Fifth Symphony?

There is no "smoking pistol" evidence that Riemann studied Beethoven's Fifth Symphony. Let us consider the matter. What is known, and it is rather indisputable, is that Riemann's closest collaborator, the man who both taught him and who worked through some of the most intimate intellectual developments with him, was Lejeune Dirichlet.[2]   And Dirichlet, as Rebecca Mendelssohn's husband and Felix Mendelssohn's brother-in-law, was steeped in classical culture and classical music. Also, Rebecca Dirichlet ran a music salon in Göttingen from 1855-1858, though it is not known which sessions Riemann attended.

But what is not so well known, and certainly not properly appreciated, is:

(a) Riemann himself played the piano.[3]

(b) In 1846, the year prior to Riemann's coming to Berlin to study under him, Dirichlet almost undoubtedly attended Felix Mendelssohn's carefully considered performance of Beethoven's Fifth Symphony. In the days and weeks after the performance, Dirichlet and Mendelssohn had, at least, a couple of dinner evenings together.

Over and above such biographical details, the coherence of Riemann's and Beethoven's methods of development of the human mind would hold. However, it is not a useless exercise to attempt a reconstruction of some of Riemann's development, before returning to the two final examples from Beethoven's Fifth.

Dirichlet and Mendelssohn on Beethoven's Fifth

What did Riemann's teacher know of Beethoven's Fifth? Mendelssohn conducted Beethoven's Fifth at Aachen on June 1, 1846. His close study of the score and careful preparation of the performance is evi-

Bernhard Riemann (1826-1866)

2. Riemann's friend, Richard Dedekind, described the relationship: "From the very beginning he [Dirichlet] felt the liveliest personal attraction toward Riemann."

3. Riemann's wife, Elise, mentions that the two of them played upon a church organ while on one of their trips in Italy. This casual mention by Elise is found in "Notes from Mrs. Professor Riemann on the last years of the life of her husband," an unpublished translation by Oyang Teng and Aaron Halevy.

denced, for example, by his discovery of an error in the printed score. Four decades earlier, Beethoven himself had complained about the mistake to the publisher, but it had never been corrected.[4]

Beethoven had been Mendelssohn's living hero from his teenage years. Along with Fanny, his older sister, Felix viewed Beethoven's late piano sonatas and late string quartets as a personal challenge that they had to master. As in the case of Gauss's *Disquisitiones Arithmeticae*, only a handful of individuals recognized and took up the challenge of Beethoven's late masterpieces. However, when Beethoven died, Felix had just turned eighteen. His death occasioned Mendelssohn's first (Op. 13) string quartet, an intensely personal work, composed around Felix's pledge to continue Beethoven's work. Further, the young Felix's study of Beethoven definitely included the Fifth Symphony. At the age of 21, Felix chose the opening movement of Beethoven's Fifth to play at the keyboard for Goethe, thinking the elderly poet needed to digest what Beethoven had accomplished.[5]

In 1846, while Mendelssohn was in Aachen as part of the South Rhine Music Festival, his brother-in-law, Dirichlet, traveled there from Berlin. He and his wife, Rebecca Mendelssohn Dirichlet, stayed in the neighboring town, Düren—the town where he had grown up. Mendelssohn conducted, along with the Fifth Symphony, his "Elijah" oratorio, and Haydn's "Creation,"[6]

Felix Mendelssohn (1809-1847)

and Mendelssohn's close friend, the famous soprano, Jenny Lind, performed and sang some of Felix's songs. Felix's sister and Dirichlet would not have missed the Festival. Then, the week after the performance of the Fifth Symphony, they dined together with Felix in Düren.[7] There is no known record as to what they discussed, but the opportunity and the likelihood of a discussion of the scientific core of Beethoven's Fifth is right there. Further, a few weeks later, back in Berlin, the Mendelssohns followed up with a second dinner with the Dirichlets.[8] There is nothing particularly surprising in the fact that Riemann's primary teacher was imbued with the cultural life of the Mendelssohn household. However, it is notable that he would have found Mendelssohn's approach to Beethoven's Fifth remarkable for the deeper implications for science and the mind—and all this, in the period when Riemann walks into his life.

Dirichlet's Student, Riemann, and His Scientific Transformation

Riemann, then twenty, began his studies with Dirichlet in Berlin in 1847, and returned to Göttingen in 1849. Riemann's close friend, Richard Dedekind, described Dirichlet's teaching method as having the ability to make "a new human being" of his students.[9]

---

4. Beethoven had two bars of music meant for a possible expanded version of the third movement, the Scherzo; but the printer included them in the non-expanded version. Beethoven wrote his publisher, August 21, 1810, to correct the matter—but it wasn't. Felix recognized the two measures were inappropriate.

5. Evidently, Goethe was both stunned and not prepared to digest what Felix was presenting: "It is tremendous but quite mad. The whole house might collapse… That does not move one at all, it only causes astonishment." Goethe's relationship with Beethoven, and with the young Mendelssohn, is fascinating, but another story entirely.

6. Curiously, Haydn's *Creation* is one of the few works that we know Riemann heard. Five years before Mendelssohn's conducting of the *Creation*, Riemann, as a fourteen-year-old, went to a performance in Hanover, along with the Kessner family.

7. They dined together at the household of Joseph and Elvira Wergifosse. Elvira sang in the Festival chorus; Joseph was a manufacturer and political activist, which included his role as a delegate to the Rhenish Diet in 1844.

8. Mendelssohn was in the midst of a related project, his setting of a part of Friedrich Schiller's "The Artist," which was premiered, a few days after the Düren dinner, in Cologne by a chorus of two thousand! The text was "Der Menschheit Würde ist in Eure Hand gegeben." This is a longer story, but any attempt to reconstruct what their discussions would have been about, rather than detracting from them, would more likely increase the likelihood of the Fifth Symphony having been part of the dialogue.

9. See the July 1856 letter located in *Eine Würdigung zu seinem 150 Geburtstag*, Braunschweig: 1981.

Amongst other matters, Dirichlet guided Riemann to the works of Gauss and Abel, securing access for Riemann to Gauss's papers in the Berlin library, and bringing unpublished works of Abel to Riemann's attention. Riemann gave special credit to Dirichlet for spending many hours with him, especially during Dirichlet's 1852 visit to Göttingen. There they worked through what would become Riemann's famous 1854 "Habilitation" presentation, "On the Hypotheses Which Form the Basis of Geometry." There we meet with Riemann's bold overturning of the fixed boundaries of over two millennia of Euclidean assumptions, hidden behind Euclid's axioms:

Lejeune Dirichlet (1805-1859)

> It is known that geometry assumes, as things given, both the notion of space and the first principles of constructions in space. She gives definitions of them which are merely nominal, while the true determinations appear in the form of axioms. The relation of these assumptions remains consequently in darkness; we neither perceive whether and how far their connection is necessary, nor *a priori*, whether it is possible. From Euclid to Legendre … this darkness was cleared up neither by mathematicians nor by such philosophers as concerned themselves with it.[10]

With this breath-taking opening, Riemann identifies the simple truth: human culture had spent over two millennia in needless obscurity regarding such basics as "the notion of space and the first principles of construction in space." Riemann's challenging task poses that one first construct a "multiply-extended manifoldness," the which may admit of variously more or less appropriate forms of measurement, or metric relations. Such manifolds are characterized by basic considerations prior to measurement, for example, what continuous pathways exist and whether they are reversible. A high priority is put upon what the mind can determine and what yet remains undetermined (and so variable)—actually, quite the Socratic approach. A manifold may transform into another "entirely different" manifold, yet it does so in a definite way, one that may be unpacked. Figuring out the dynamical relations of these transformations of various dimensionalities is more than, for example, figuring out tricks for factoring 2nd-power equations into two 1st-power equations.

It was Gauss who, in 1849, had emphasized for Riemann that the "higher domain of the abstract theory of magnitudes" should be developed, dealing with "combinations among magnitudes linked by continuity." This investigation, prior to any determination of metrical relations, was called by Gauss's student, J. B. Listing, "Topologie." However, of note, Riemann still preferred to identify it by Leibniz's term, *"analysis situs."*

The extent of Riemann's Leibnizian core is not fully appreciated. For example, his first fourteen years with his family in the quiet countryside are usually overlooked. But his father fought in the Liberation Wars against Napoleon, and his beloved mother was the daughter and grand-daughter of Leibnizians. The grandfather, Georg Wilhelm Ebell, introduced Leibniz's proposal on fire-fighting into London, and the father, Georg August Ebell, was a longtime associate at Göttingen of Leibnizian Georg Lichtenberg. Lacking further knowledge of the warm familial ties of Riemann's childhood, one can still infer a solid moral underpinning, which was characteristic of Riemann's scientific passion. Whether the method is called *"analysis situs"* or *"topological,"* Riemann brought Leibniz's methodology to a high pitch, as part of his passion for maturely dealing with the rich complexities of life.

Riemann's Violinist and His Work on the Ear

Riemann's other main connection to Mendelssohn addresses, in a somewhat different fashion, Riemann's

---

10. Find Riemann's dissertation at http://archive.larouchepac.com/node/12479.

passion for the issues of thinking, hearing and music. One of Riemann's last projects, one that he chose even as he knew he was dying, was in response to a reductionist account of music and of hearing produced by Hermann Helmholtz. Riemann objected to the trivializing of the power of the ear and of music, insisting that any analysis of such a fascinating part of nature had to rise up to the level of the experience. The same methodology he employed in investigating dynamics in the infinitesimally small, needed to be brought to bear to account for the incredible powers of discrimination of the hearing process.[11]

Riemann's collaborator on his paper on the workings of the ear

Jacob Henle (1809-1885)

was Göttingen's professor of physiology, Jacob Henle. An associate of Mendelssohn, he had even considered a pursuit of marriage with Felix's older sister, Fanny—that is, before he discovered she was already engaged. A few items, arranged chronologically from Henle's life, give an idea of Riemann's colleague on his last project. Henle studied violin under Beethoven's colleague, Rudolph Kreutzer.[12] He organized a musical salon in Göttingen, called the "Friday Night Club," several years before Rebecca Dirichlet arrived in Göttingen. Performers included the violinist Joseph Joachim. And of note, Riemann and/or his friend Dedekind drew Henle's attention to Gauss's *Disquisitiones Arithmeti-*

cae, prior to the work on the ear.

Henle published Riemann's last work in the physiology journal that he had founded. Henle contrasted Riemann's approach to Helmholtz's fundamentalism: "Riemann thought that the mathematical problem to be solved was in fact a hydraulic one." Riemann focused upon the interface between the air fluid and the inner ear fluid, in addressing the qualitative event: "If we take "timbre" to mean the quality of sound … then this is evidently communicated by the apparatus with complete fidelity, so long as it transmits to the fluid of the inner ear the variation in air pressure at every moment at a constant ratio of amplification … Were the timbre curve noticeably altered, such sensitivity of hearing as indicated by, for example, the perception of slight differences of pronunciation, would seem to me scarcely conceivable…" For Riemann, the scientific investigation began with the miraculous fact that the dynamics of the quality of sound accomplished what it actually did. If the hydraulics of the inner ear could track variations in air pressure (from sound transmission) so rapidly and so accurately, then the mathematical language had to rise to the level of the rich phenomena. When Henle published Riemann's work, it was still unfinished, as Riemann had died before finishing it.

---

11. Three examples: The hairs in the cochlea function on the order of a few atomic radii. At normal conversation levels, the oscillation of the basal membrane is no larger than an atomic radius. The amount of energy in a barely audible musical tone is about twice the energy of a single photon of light. No other human sense comes close to these levels. See Robert Gallagher's "Riemann and the Göttingen School of Physiology" in *Fusion* magazine, Volume 6, No. 3 (Sept/Oct 1984) http://wlym.com/archive/fusion/fusion/19840910- fusion.pdf

12. Henle, like Mendelssohn, was from a Jewish family, one that had converted so that they could pursue their professions. On a visit to Henle's home, Mendelssohn charmed Henle's sister with a private performance of his "Midsummer Night's Dream" overture. Mendelssohn and Henle socialized off-and-on, including in the period prior to Felix's performance of Beethoven's Fifth Symphony. Henle's scientific work greatly impressed Alexander Humboldt, and it was Humboldt who had personally intervened to free Henle, at a time when he had been given a six-year prison term for political activities.

III. Twelve Boring Notes—or Riemann's Thought-Mass?

What to make of Beethoven reaching into his audience's mind, surgically detaching the metrical and prosodic (or topological) components, and re-attaching them in reverse order? Nowhere does Beethoven's grasp of such powerful matters show themselves in this work as in his gripping sixteen-note melody, where the first twelve notes are all the same note.

One may hear this at 00:30-00:36 of the third movement of https://www.youtube.com/watch?v=mCnfX9obJ3M. Okay, what is so gripping? It certainly was not the richness of tonal development. Sixteen notes, grouped in four two-measure segments, each of four notes. We had that opening, four-note germ of an idea—but now, with the tonal motion (G-E♭) stripped out and only the single note, G, left. A veritable kaleidoscope of rich interconnections ensues.

On one level, we have the four-note germ played three times in succession, as three of one "thing," followed by the one of another "thing"—here, four changing tones, or what we used to recognize as melodic material. With total efficiency of statement, with total command of the workings of the mind, we now get a multiplicity of both the "sss-l" prosody and the "3:1" metrical relation. Both the prosodic and the metrical are in play, but on more than one level. The first three two-measure segments can be heard as one long six-measure event, against the short, last two-measure segment. (In this incarnation, it reminds us of the second theme of the first movement, covered above.) But now, the last two-measure segment is distinguished by its "melodic" motion. It is the "change" from the "sameness" of the twelve repeated G's. So, now "sameness" is associated with the "long," in contrast to the opening four notes of the first movement, where the three same notes were the three short events.

Re-hearing the gripping sixteen notes, we can also hear the eight measures as a four-fold expansion of the original two-measure idea, and this suggests each of the three two-measure segments are also a "short" and the last two-measure segment is a "long"—or, if not actually "long," still as related to the original "long" by its characteristic changing notes. This last relationship we will examine a bit further when we take up the third and last example from the Fifth Symphony, regarding the matter of where language comes from, and why there are determinative shapes of ideas prior to their incarnation in actual words. The whole opening movement is replete with a wealth of variegated readings of the two fundamental relationships. The core issue here, with this 16-note version, is the wealth of riches that Beethoven mines, once he has so powerfully demarcated the prosodic and metrical qualities. So, it never was a matter of twelve of the same, boring notes.

Riemann was fascinated with the possibility of mining such riches. Reflect on Beethoven's gripping sixteen-note passage when considering Riemann's de-

scription of the dynamics of his "thought-masses": "As they are forming, the thought-masses blend; or are folded together, or connect to one another and also to older thought-masses, in a precisely determined manner. The character and strength of these connections depend upon causes which were only partially recognized by Herbart, but which I shall fill out in what follows. They rest primarily on the internal relationships among the thought-masses." Furthermore, he was confident regarding the healthy development of the personality based upon such dynamics: "The mind is a compact, multiply-connected thought-mass with internal connections of the most intimate kind. It grows continuously as new thought masses enter it, and this is the means by which it continues to develop." At this point, before proceeding, it might be best to put down this article and take eight minutes to listen to the first movement: https://www.youtube.com/watch?v=xmwHOhSYJl4. (The link is to a 1937 performance by Wilhelm Furtwängler; and he is, indeed, one of those rare conductors who phrases the second theme of the first movement correctly!)

The circumstances of Beethoven's decision to develop his Fifth Symphony are worth one quick snapshot. Beethoven began work on his Fifth Symphony in 1804, three years after Gauss had completed his *Disquisitiones Arithmeticae*. He had just finished his massive, and revolutionary, Third Symphony, called the *Eroica*, a work that was not easily received. (Though the Fourth Symphony was begun after he had begun work on the Fifth, it was published prior to the Fifth.) One notable figure, Prince Louis Ferdinand of Prussia, was captivated by the *Eroica*.[13] Evidently, he had "listened to it with tense attention which grew with every movement" and had demanded that the symphony be repeated. Louis Ferdinand came to Vienna to visit with Beethoven. Coincidentally—or perhaps not—the Prince was the cousin of Gauss's sponsor, Duke Carl of Brunswick.[14] The discussions with Beethoven in 1804 were most fruitful. Louis Ferdinand's championing of the *Eroica*

---

13. While Beethoven had no problem with great men making history, he was disgusted by Napoleon's proclaiming himself Emperor, and tore up his original dedication of the Third Symphony. The Prince shared Beethoven's view of Napoleon, loved the symphony, and mobilized Germany against the Emperor.

14. They were actually both grandsons of Leibniz's student, Sophie Dorothea, Queen of Prussia, and great-grandsons of Leibniz's patroness, Sophie. Tragically, they both died leading the fight against Napoleon's invasion in the Fall of 1806.

gave Beethoven's novel work a new life. Beethoven recognized the role of Louis Ferdinand in defending his *Eroica* and dedicated his C Minor Pianoforte Concerto to the Prince, a fine pianist.[15] And a re-enthused Beethoven began his C Minor Symphony project, the Fifth Symphony.

IV. The Formation of Ideas, and Singing

One of the provocative results of the 16-note example was the last point, that the last four notes, after twelve G's in a row, suggest that melody is born out of prosody. Once Beethoven had isolated two different, though related, powers of the mind, he made this higher-level interplay of prosody and metrics the basis of composition, and this is where the mind sings. The third example deals with this.

The most singular feature of the symphony, after the opening, motivic four notes, is perhaps the oboe "cadenza." Usually it is assumed that the genius Beethoven simply has eccentricities, such as having the orchestra come to a crashing halt, while the oboe inserts a mini-cadenza into the symphony—a bit of melodic relief after all the non-lyrical material. What could Beethoven possibly be doing?[16]

Early in the first movement (measures 19-21), the orchestra makes a crashing statement with three massive chords—but Beethoven has the first violins simply hold on to their G after everyone else has ended the chord. It is as if they had something to say, but had lost their train of thought. But after a timeless moment, they do stop, everyone looks the other way, and matters proceed. But at the parallel part in the recapitulation (measure 268, or 04:46-05:00 in the Furtwängler recording), emerging out of the crashing chord, a lone oboe transforms the explosive, rather percussive chord; it extends the note, and then softens and shapes the single note. A melodic sug-

gestion emerges, G-F-E♭, F-E♭-D-E♭ F-E♭-D. Out of all the forceful developments, a butterfly surprisingly emerges … and then it is gone. The melodic notes? Why, they are the same as the forceful, opening "non-melody" of sss-l: G-E♭, F-D. Beethoven has, very late in the movement, provided us with the "sung" version, one that could have melted our hearts. But he provides it only long enough to suggest such simple beauties as an afterthought. Immediately, he pulls us back into his maelstrom of relentless developments.

But now think back to that held chord, with the G on top. At first, presented so forcefully by the full orchestra, it even takes a moment for the ear to hear it as a stable tone, before the massive chord fades away, and the sound of the lone oboe emerges. The percussive event takes on length and shape with the oboe, and, if done properly, a natural vibrato develops as the tone takes on life. The oboe's melody has begun while still on the held G—and only then unwrapping itself melodically into the other notes. The percussive singularity unfolds a flowing continuity. To state it a bit too succinctly, Beethoven is working where language itself takes shape—where continuous, melodic shapes, which we call "vowels," are bounded by discontinuous, percussive "stops," which we call consonants. Thus, Beethoven's simple directions, inside the geography of the brain: Just go to where the metrical arises out of the prosodic shape, the gestalt, and you'll find where melody and language are born!

It is not terribly easy to use words to describe how thought-masses work prior to language. However, the wilful act of refusing to stigmatize Beethoven as an eccentric, or to characterize him as the type of genius where one simply has to look the other way at certain embarrassing moments, is a beginning—where one can begin to hear what the man is thinking. Riemann was possessed by a similar passion to make the healthiest, happiest movements of his mind transparent, to actually give determination to his determinable thought-masses.

---

15. The compositions of Louis Ferdinand that this author has heard are quite good, better than that of any other nobility. Beethoven is said to have commented: "Now and then there are pretty bits in them." Thayer reports that Beethoven complimented the Prince: his playing "was not that of a king or prince but more like that of a thoroughly good pianoforte player."

16. Peter Schickele fashioned a hilarious "send-up" of Beethoven's "eccentricity." See http://www.youtube.com/watch?v=l0vHpeUO5mw, around 4:40—5:00.

V. Determination

The striking opening of Riemann's composition, clearing away a couple of millennia of lazy and wishful delusions, can be repeated in the experience of hearing Beethoven's Fifth, but without all the accumulated baggage; that is, hearing what the living Beethoven would have you discover about the powers of your own mind. This is not an esoteric subject for mathematicians and/or musicians. Indeed, a closely related experience is that of thinking through what the establishment of a nation as "a beacon of hope and temple of liberty" should have accomplished in the world, and how what has been determinable might now become determined. Indeed, the very ability to characterize the present moment in history, and to have that characterization be known to be on solid footing—more solid than the pretense of all the primitive, "Euclidean" methods of establishing supposed "solidity"—is a cultural and scientific gift from Beethoven and Riemann. The ability to craft appropriate measure-relations amongst the various cultures signing up for the "win-win" approach of Chinese President Xi Jinping, is a cultural and scientific gift from Helga and Lyndon LaRouche. Use such gifts wisely. Become determined to make what is determinable, determined.

Société Wilhelm Furtwängler

Wilhelm Furtwängler conducting in Paris in 1934.

Trump, Xi, and the New Opportunity For Humanity

This is an edited transcript of Helga Zepp-LaRouche's webcast of Nov. 9.

Harley Schlanger: Hello, I'm Harley Schlanger from the Schiller Institute and I'd like to welcome you to this week's webcast, featuring Schiller Institute Chairwoman Helga Zepp-LaRouche.

Obviously, the lead topic for today, is the historic visit of President Donald Trump to China, as part of his extended visit to Asia. Now, if you're looking for reporting on this in the Western media, forget it. Just look at some of the headlines—the *Washington Post* had a headline today, "How Will China Play Trump?" The *New York Times* featured an Obama Deputy National Security Advisor, Tony Blinken—of Winken, Blinken and Nod—and Blinken had a comment, whose title was "Trump Ceding Global Leadership to China." And you have the Democratic Senator from Connecticut, Richard Blumenthal coming out in a press conference, accusing Trump of "colluding" with China.

So we really need to get a picture of what's happening and its full strategic significance, and for that we turn to Helga Zepp-LaRouche.

Helga Zepp-LaRouche: Hello. I think from what I know know today, which is the second day of what I would call an historic visit of President Trump to China—I think it is exactly what I expected would happen: That both sides know perfectly well that the future of mankind depends on the relationship between the United States and China, as *the* most important two nuclear powers and economic powers in the world. And I think it went very well. The statements by President

Xinhua/Rao Aimin

China President Xi Jinping (left), in a moment of the grand ceremony to welcome U.S. President Donald Trump on the square outside the East Gate of the Great Hall of the People in Beijing, China, Nov. 9, 2017.

Xi Jinping characterizing the meeting as a strategic new beginning, a mutually beneficial relationship of historic importance which can solve not only the problems of the two peoples, but of the whole world—I think this is absolutely to the point. And President Trump was very enthusiastic: He praised China and its great President, for whom, according to his Tweet, he has very warm feelings—this is really good. Because if the two Presidents understand each other and can make it work, then I fully agree, there is no problem in the world which cannot be tackled.

So I think this is a gigantic step forward, and I think it's also interesting that Trump, who has spoken a lot about the trade gap between the United States and China, said nevertheless that he does not blame China for it, because he understands that President Xi has done everything he could for the maximum benefit of

Xinhua/Li Xueren

President Xi (2nd from left), his wife Peng Liyuan (1st on left), and U.S. President Trump and his wife Melania Trump watch a performance at the Great Hall of the People in Beijing, that was part of the grand ceremony to welcome the Trumps Nov. 9, 2017.

his own country and people. Instead, Trump blamed previous U.S. Administrations for having allowed this trade gap now to have come about. And remember, the Chinese have always wanted to import much more from the United States, but the previous administrations, which pursued a confrontation, containment, and encirclement policy towards China, refused to sell many of the products which China had wanted to buy, with the pretext that they had "dual use." They claimed they could be used both for civilian and military purpose—but of course, you can use almost anything for either peaceful or not so peaceful purposes, depending on the intent of your policy.

So I think this is very good. They concluded, I think, somewhere in the range of $250 billion in deals, ranging from infrastructure, transport, and energy, to agricultural exports from the United States to China—just a very wide variety of economic deals. They also decided to not only improve and strengthen the relationship between the two Presidents, but to increase the cooperation on all levels, and to strengthen the four permanent dialogues which had been arranged in Florida in April, one of them dealing with economic cooperation. And I think all of the basis has been laid to

continue to develop this relationship to the benefit, not only of China and the United States, but really for the whole world.

They agreed fully on the need to solve the North Korea problem, on which they want to work together, and Trump also expressed his confidence that with the help of China, and Russia, as he said earlier, that the problem can be brought to a positive solution.

While I have not seen any direct mention of the United States working with the Belt and Road Initiative as such, I know that that is the mindset of President Xi, and I also think that coming out of the 19th Congress of the Communist Party of China, where Xi Jinping has set the goal of building a "community of a shared future of mankind" by 2050—that this trip by President Trump has been a gigantic step in the right direction. And I think the Chinese really know how to make conscious to visitors the 5,000-year history of China, and that Trump was really treated very well. They had a one-day or several hour special tour of the Forbidden City, which was closed to the public, and they performed three Beijing operas, and showed him the restoration of ancient artifacts. So Trump was very, very happy, and he sent a message to Xi Jinping saying that

White House/Andrea Hanks

Japan's Prime Minister Shinzo Abe (left) greets President Trump and First Lady Melania Trump on Nov. 6, 2017, on the Japan leg of Trump's Asia tour.

White House/Andrea Hanks

Above, President Trump (center rear, waving) participates with other leaders of the region in the Asia-Pacific Economic Cooperation (APEC) meeting in Da Nang, Vietnam, Nov. 10-11, 2017.

At right, President Trump at the APEC summit talking to President Xi (right). Viet Nam President Tran Dai Quang, (2nd from left) and Singapore Prime Minister Lee Hsien Loong (3rd from left).

White House/Andrea Hanks

Korea and Japan. I wonder if you have some thoughts about those meetings and their significance?

Zepp-LaRouche: I think they were significant, but I think the upcoming meeting in Vietnam is going to be more important. Trump may meet with President Putin tomorrow, and I think that meeting will also be very important. Because President Putin just wrote an article ahead of that APEC summit, where he said that what will be discussed at the APEC meeting, in the context of the already-ongoing integration of the Belt and Road Initiative with the Eurasian Economic Union, is the Russian presentation of a major plan for the development of the Far East of Russia. This will be a national priority for the 21st Century, where many infrastructure projects are to be built, but also industrial parks and other investments; and he emphasized the positive cooperation among Russia, China, Japan, and the Koreas.

So I think what is clearly emerging, is more and more an integrated new economic system, where basically it is very clear, that as long as the Europeans, or at least the EU and the German government, remain in their stand-offish attitude—it is as one businessman said recently, "if they don't jump onto the train, then they will see the lights of the caboose leaving the station, and they'll be left behind."

The center of strategic importance is clearly moving towards Asia right now. And hopefully this U.S.-Chinese relationship will continue to expand.

Schlanger: And one other thing I'd like you to comment on, I'm sure it's very interesting to you, given the importance that you put on the cultural exchange and the understanding of other cultures, is President Trump's [six-year-old] granddaughter singing Chinese songs to them on video. Did you get a chance to see

he and Melania will never forget this experience. So I think this is very positive from a human standpoint.

And these journalists should just be ashamed of themselves. They are so cynical that nothing ever moves their hearts and minds, and probably these minds are dried out like old prunes anyway—so I wouldn't worry about what they're writing. I think these two presidents have made a very positive step, moving human history forward.

Schlanger: It's also significant that there is a group of businessmen who are part of the delegation that will be involved in meetings, and I think that's where we may hear later, more of the specifics on the Belt and Road connection with the Chinese.

Now, before Trump came to China, he was in South

CIA Director Mike Pompeo

that, Helga?

Zepp-LaRouche: Yes, yes. I think this was very sweet, and obviously while the little girl was not there, her video was presented, and I think it expressed a spirit of profound appreciation for Mandarin culture, and I think it was very well taken.

Schlanger: Now, when you talk about the journalists with their nonsense in their coverage of this, and attempting to keep the real story out, you are seeing some breaks with the whole Russia-gate story. And of course, we've been covering this very extensively, but in the last couple of days there was the report that Bill Binney, the former NSA technical expert, met with Mike Pompeo of the CIA at Donald Trump's urging; Pompeo talked with him, at Trump's urging, to discuss the fact that there was actually no Russian hacking. What do you make of that?

'Russiagate' Lies Exposed

Zepp-LaRouche: I think this is very important. It clearly shows that President Trump is fully aware of the revelations of the Veteran Intelligence Professionals for Sanity (VIPS), of which William Binney is a member, and that means that President Trump is also not afraid of Russia-gate. Because by asking Pompeo, the current head of the CIA, to meet with Binney, that is now on the record, so to speak, and now the investigation which the FBI never did, obviously has to follow. And the key ar-

dd/Tim Pierce

Donna Brazile

gument which Binney made previously at our event in New York and on other occasions, is that there is forensic evidence that there was no hacking, but rather this material was downloaded on site to a storage device, because the speed with which it occurred is four times higher than you could get from the Internet. And the VIPS presented this documentation at a Schiller Institute event in New York a couple of months ago. That will now be investigated, and they will come to exactly the same conclusion, that there was no hacking, and with that I think the whole Russia "spook" story will just vanish.

And that will liberate Trump to carry out policy as a President should do. The whole purpose of the Russia-gate, was to prevent him from making a change in the attitude towards Russia and China. I think this is clearly backfiring.

And then, you have all these investigations now, which we mentioned last week, with the Donna Brazile book, saying very clearly that Hillary did steal the election, in a way. In a certain sense, this whole story can turn totally the other way: There are the ongoing investigations in the Senate and in the Congress on the British role [in interfering in the 2016 election], which is now becoming much more prominent in the discussion—that U.S. intelligence services from the Obama period used foreign intelligence against a U.S. Presidential opponent—I mean, that's more than "opposition research," it's potentially something very criminal. And that may all come out now.

Schlanger: Two other footnotes on that: One is that Binney referred to Russia-gate as "mindless drivel," and if you think about it, that's what the American people and the people in Western Europe have been fed for a full year now—mindless drivel.

Now, the other thing that I think is interesting, is the interconnection between the Hillary Clinton exposé from Donna Brazile and the whole Fusion GPS story, because this story is now coming out of all the interconnection, leading back to London. So, as you've been pointing out, it looks as though this whole thing will come to the forefront soon.

Zepp-LaRouche: There is another interesting thing, which I think people should reflect upon. Because all these accusations against Putin as a dictator, against Xi Jinping as a "new Mao," and all of these insinuations that these countries are not democratic and are dictatorships—well, look at the Democratic Party, and I emphasize *Democratic* Party—it now is established that the DNC picked their candidate, Hillary Clinton, one year before the national convention, and then manipulated the whole electoral process in such a way that Bernie Sanders, who probably would have won against Trump,—or at least there was a good chance that this could have happened—was sidelined, and obviously betrayed.

Now, what does that say about "democracy"? I think people should reflect on the fact that this present party system, as it has developed with the very large influence of Wall Street in it—given the fact that people need $5 million, $10 million in order to run for a Congressional seat—that system clearly is not working. And I think it is time to change a lot of things, to change not only the set of relations among nations internationally, but also to go back to a discussion like that in the *Federalist Papers* in the United States, for example: Can a people govern itself? I think this is a very important question, and I think this democracy is just a joke. The Democratic Party did their very best to prove exactly that.

Schlanger: We're also learning more and more about how this was an operation to take money from the state parties, and that's one of the reasons the Democrats have been losing every race until recently. Interesting, also, I think, just to make a note of this, is that Donna Brazile referred to "three titanic egos," those of Hillary Clinton, Barack Obama, and Debbie Wasserman Schultz, stripping the core out of the Democratic Party, and I think that's what most people see.

Now, Helga, the other thing I think is really crucial that we need to hear your thoughts on, is what's happening in the Middle East right now. As is typically the case, when there are developments like the Trump-Xi Jinping meeting, the enemy is operating elsewhere to cause serious disruptions. We see the events unfolding in Lebanon, with a possible Saudi-Israeli involvement in a war in Lebanon and the ongoing events in Yemen. You just participated in a conference a couple days ago via video, in Yemen, about the Chinese Silk Road extension to that part of the Arabian Peninsula. Why don't you give us a little bit of a report on that, and what your thoughts are about this very dangerous situation emerging in the Middle East?

Zepp-LaRouche: It is very dangerous because just at the point when the ISIS forces were as good as defeated in Syria and Iraq, you had this operation, obviously run by the young Crown Prince Mohammad bin Salman, where, when Prime Minister Saad Hariri of Lebanon was on a visit in Saudi Arabia, conveniently U.S. intelligence—at least that's what some Israeli reports are saying—provided Saudi Arabia with the information that there was an assassination plot against Hariri, so he resigned and stayed in Saudi Arabia. And that naturally aggravates the situation in Lebanon, which is *very* tense anyway, because this country has as many refugees as it has citizens, which means a totally tense situation as it is.

Obviously, then there was this strange incident about a missile, shot from Yemen into Saudi Arabia—now that is very strange, because what would be the purpose of one single missile? Naturally, the Saudis claim that it was from Iran via Hezbollah, and that is now heating up the whole situation. The worst thing about it, is that the Saudis blockaded all ports and entry points into Yemen. This has dramatically worsened the situation in Yemen, which is already one of absolute danger of starvation of millions of people—so that even the UN Human Rights Commission and others came out and said there is an *immediate* danger of seven million people dying of hunger and epidemics, cholera, and similar things in Yemen, and that they demand that all ports and other such routes be opened immediately and the blockade be ended.

I think this is something which must get international attention—because this is genocide taking place before the world public—and this absolutely must end.

And we should not forget that the dossier which we published about Robert Mueller, which details that the apparatus which went after my husband and his organization in the '80s and '90s, is the same apparatus which is covering up for 9/11, and is the apparatus which is still deploying against President Trump. And these are absolutely forces similar to those behind this operation against Yemen.

So all this hangs together, and requires absolute, important investigation. People have to really get mobilized, so this genocide is stopped.

Schlanger: And in spite of the desperate situation in Yemen, it seems from the report I saw—the conference you addressed a couple of days ago—there's tremendous spirit. Again, the optimism of the New Silk Road is coming into that country, isn't it?

Zepp-LaRouche: Yes, yes. There is a very delightful reading group. People have been studying the report which we published, *The New Silk Road Becomes the World Land-Bridge*, for quite some time. That obviously includes the extension of the New Silk Road into Yemen. And people are really taking this as the hope for their future.

I think it would be very good if people in other countries around the world would do likewise, because there *is* this alternative plan! And the chances are that it will lead to cooperation among Russia, China, and the United States, in rebuilding the region, getting Iran and Saudi Arabia to the table and overcoming this terrible conflict between the Sunnis and the Shi'ites, which has been played by the British for a very long time; and that we move to a different era of mankind. I think this is the imperative demand of the hour.

Schlanger: And just to come back to the overriding theme of the U.S.-Russia-China relationship, I guess we'll see that again in action, with the meetings still to come in Vietnam and the Philippines, that President Trump is going to have on his trip.

Zepp-LaRouche: Yes. I think that that will be tomorrow, so people should pay attention to this summit, because I think major things will occur there.

Second Chance for Mankind

Schlanger: I just wanted to bring another thing to the attention of our listeners: This has been a week of anniversaries, and I think it's important to get a good, competent historical perspective of what's happened. You had just a couple days ago, the 100th anniversary of the Balfour Declaration, which has a lot to do with the British Empire's destruction of the Middle East and the ongoing activity there. There was the 100th anniversary of the Bolshevik Revolution yesterday. And then today, is a very important day in Germany: It's the

EIRNS/Dean Andromidas
Lyndon LaRouche at his press conference in West Berlin, Oct. 22, 1988.

28th anniversary of the fall of the Berlin Wall, and you were very active in that period. In fact, I think it's fair to say that the idea of the Silk Road grew out of the effects of the collapse of the Berlin Wall and the potential with the reunification of Germany.

So I'd like you to say something about that, because you are uniquely situated to put this history together in a way that makes sense for people.

Zepp-LaRouche: Well, yes, that is absolutely true. My husband, Lyndon LaRouche, had forecast the collapse of the Soviet Union in 1984. He then said that if they stuck to their then-existing policies of the Ogarkov Plan and similar things, and to primitive accumulation against their own economy, they would collapse in five years. And that's exactly what started to happen with the fall of the Wall. Then he forecast in 1988, that the Comecon would collapse soon—he made that prognosis in '88, one year before it happened—and that there would be soon German unification with Berlin as the capital, and that a unified Germany should start to develop the countries of the Comecon, with modern technology and infrastructure. He proposed the first such country should be Poland.

So therefore, when the Wall came down, it was not really a surprise for us. As a matter of fact, we were the only ones prepared for that occasion, and we developed the idea of a Productive Triangle of Paris-Berlin-Vienna, which was a highly industrialized area of the size in territory of, let's say, Japan. We proposed it should be upgraded through infrastructure, maglev trains, HTR nuclear reactors, the Sänger project for sub-orbital Mach 1-2 planes. We proposed that, and we were ready when the Soviet Union then collapsed—as a matter of fact, we had that report ready in January of 1990, about six weeks after the fall of the Wall.

This would have been a peace plan at that point. But as we know, the powers that be, the neo-cons in the United States, Margaret Thatcher, Mitterrand in France— they all had their own geopolitical reasons to prevent that. But when the Soviet Union collapsed in '91, we just extended the Productive Triangle concept to the Eurasian Land-Bridge, proposing economic transportation development corridors along the Trans-

Fall of the Berlin Wall, 1989.

Siberian Railway, and along the old Silk Road. What is happening now with China and the Belt and Road Initiative could have happened in 1991.

It didn't happen. I published documentation about the developments from that time, which is called "The Lost Chance of 1989," because that opportunity was not used. People remember that "shock therapy" was imposed on Russia, in order to turn Russia from a superpower into a Third World, raw materials-exporting country, which was what happened in the Yeltsin period. And so this entire decade of the '90s was one of genocide for Russia, and people have written books about that, including Prof. Sergey Glazyev and others.

Now, when Putin came in, he started to undo that, and that is why he attracted so much hatred from people who had wanted to put Russia into a corner. He is now doing a lot to undo that, and what I said earlier about the development of the Russian Far East, is a very important component of it.

So in a certain sense, this is the second chance. This time I think the possibility that it will be used to establish a true peace order for the 21st century, ending the period of geopolitics, is very close. If the relationship which was clearly brought forward in a gigantic way between Xi Jinping and Trump, if that consolidates as the relationship between China, Russia, and hopefully the United States as part of that triangle, then maybe India will change its mind, and maybe even the Europeans will get onboard. We can enter a completely new set of relationships among countries.

And I invite all of you, our viewers, to become an active part of this. The Schiller Institute is a membership think tank. You can become an active member in the Schiller Institute, by contributing research, by doing all kinds of things. You can actually help to bring such a new era of civilization about, by joining us: So I want to invite you do exactly that, to celebrate the moment.

Schlanger: And I think you made very clear to people, how devastating losing that opportunity of 1989 has been—with the 28 years of degeneration in the United States, the wars, the terrorism and so on—we *have* to take this chance. And this is where the optimism comes from, that there are countries that are already doing that.

Zepp-LaRouche: Yes. It will sink in, that that situation is there, and if the Russia-gate in the United States stops, I think the world can become better. And even in the United States, people can join this hopeful perspective. And I think they need it so badly, because the infrastructure is in terrible shape, the drug epidemic is there; in Europe you have a situation where many youth, especially in the south of Europe, have neither a job nor an education. But with the New Silk Road, people have a future and a perspective to really *end* poverty, to end the miserable life for so many, and focus on the common aims of mankind. There are so many riches to be discovered, so many discoveries to be made. It's about time that we give mankind an order which is worthy of the character of the human species.

Schlanger: Well, the next few days will be very important, and I think it's very important that people join us again next week to get the update on the completion of President Trump's trip' and the implications for us in the West.

So Helga, thank you very much for joining us, and for all of you listening, we'll see you next week.

Zepp-LaRouche: Yes, until next week.

Extending the New Silk Road to West Asia and Africa

The following is taken from the upcoming Schiller Institute Special Report Extending the New Silk Road to West Asia and Africa: A Vision of an Economic Renaissance, *authored by Hussein Askary and Jason Ross. We print below an abbreviated Table of Contents and the full Introduction. To be notified when the report is available for purchase, please email* schiller@schillerinstitute.org

TABLE OF CONTENTS

Introduction

Global media coverage of Africa and the Middle East (or, rather, Southwest Asia[1]) typically focuses on war, terrorism, famine, epidemics, and mass immigration. Very seldom are these two regions associated with economic development, scientific breakthroughs, or cultural advancements.

Unfortunately, this image of the region has a substantial basis in reality. The situation does have domestic causes, but is also largely related to global geopolitical factors and the attempt by major global powers to secure spheres of influence, natural resources, markets, and strategic and political advantages against other global and regional adversaries.

But, the purpose of this report is not to dwell on all the ills that have contributed to this reality (something that the authors of this report and their associates have extensively dealt with in other publications). Rather, our mission here is to find and show the way forward out of the current, admittedly very dangerous, situation.

A New Global Paradigm

The good news is that a new paradigm in world politics has emerged, and is concretely changing the rules

---

1. The authors prefer not to use the term "Middle East" for two reasons: 1. It is not a scientific term, because geographical regions should be divided into subsections of continents, and not into regions seen from the visual or political perspective of one part of the world or another. Therefore, the correct term to be used to designate this region is "Southwest Asia" or, for the purposes of this report, "West Asia"; 2. The term "Middle East" is part of the legacy of the British Empire, and was coined by the British India Office in the 1850s, to distinguish the different "properties" of the Empire as they were geographically imagined from London's perspective. See Beaumont, Peter; Blake, Gerald H.; and Wagstaff, J. Malcolm, *The Middle East: A Geographical Study* (1988).

BRICS leaders at the 6th summit in Fortaleza, Brazil. Left to right: Russia President Vladimir Putin, India Prime Minister Narendra Modi, Brazil President Dilma Rousseff, China President Xi Jinping, and South Africa President Jacob Zuma.

President Xi Jinping (left) and his counterpart in Kazakhstan, Nursultan Nazarbayev, at the ceremony in Astana where Xi proposed the Belt and Road Initiative, Sept 7, 2013.

of the game of what can be called the old paradigm—the paradigm responsible for the above-mentioned problems in West Asia and Africa.

This new paradigm is not a plan to be undertaken in the future, nor is it a hypothetical, academic speculation. It is a reality taking hold in the world now. While this new paradigm has been in the making for many years, it has been given concrete expression over the past four years in two interrelated events:

1. The announcement of the One Belt, One Road Initiative (or Belt and Road Initiative—henceforth referred to as BRI) by Chinese President Xi Jinping in late 2013,[2] which was a breakthrough for the New Silk Road policy adopted by China since 1996. President Xi's initiative transformed the policy into a global strategy backed by the massive financial, technological and political power that China had developed in the previous 20 years of fast-track industrialization, hinging on the construction of infrastructure mega-projects whose scale had not been seen in the world since the U.S. New Deal before World War II, the post-World War II reconstruction of Germany, and the U.S. space program of the 1960s.

2. The July 2014 Fortaleza Declaration by the BRICS nations (Brazil, Russia, India, China and South Africa).[3] This declaration cemented the economic and financial cooperation among these nations, envisaging the joint creation of new financial institutions, such as the New Development Bank, that are almost solely focused on development of infrastructure, trade, industry, scientific cooperation and research. What these nations, especially China, have proven, is that eliminating poverty, famine, and disease can only be achieved by full-scale industrialization and the utilization of state-of-the-art technologies to unleash the creative, productive powers of society, as the United States and Europe had done in previous centuries, and not by piecemeal small steps, as the United States and Europe have been proposing for Africa and Asia since at least the 1960s, or by "humanitarian," emergency aid, for example, which has become the rule, rather than the exception in dealing with Africa. The BRICS nations, with China foremost among them, have even redefined what was called "sustainable development," using the phrase to mean industrialization, food security, and the eradication of poverty, rather than adjusting the living standards of people to immediately available

---

2. President Xi Jinping announced the creation of the "Economic Belt of the Silk Road" in a speech in the Nazarbayev University in Astana, Kazakhstan in September 2013. The Belt is a land-based economic corridor extending from eastern China to western Europe and engaging 69 nations in its path. One month later he announced, from Jakarta, Indonesia, the intention to launch the 21st Century Maritime Silk Road together with other nations. This includes building numerous ports on the sea lanes of the Pacific and Indian Oceans and the Mediterranean. The two projects complement each other and together make up the BRI. http://english.gov.cn/beltAndRoad/

3. See http://brics.itamaraty.gov.br/media2/press-rele ases/214-sixth-brics-summit-fortaleza-declaration

China Round Table of leaders at the Belt and Road International Forum in Beijing, May 15, 2017.

resources and technology. Technological apartheid had for many years been a policy practiced under various excuses by industrial nations, preventing developing nations from acquiring advanced technologies. Now, the BRICS nations, led by China, are breaking that "rule," making advanced technology available for nations in Asia and Africa.

These developments come as the western world has entered into the worst financial and physical-economic crisis since the Great Depression, weakening its ability to resist and to undermine the rising economic power of the BRICS, a response that would be expected based on the geopolitical trends of the past. Although seen as a challenge by many in the crisis-ridden, formerly industrialized nations, or the OECD nations, living within what can be called "the old paradigm," the new paradigm is in reality an inclusive process, not an exclusive club of developing nations. The United States, the European Union (EU), and Japan are frequently invited by China, Russia, and India to join the process of development that the latter nations are involved in, both within their own territories and around the world.

The May 14-15, 2017 Beijing Belt and Road Forum for International Cooperation,[4] was the proof of success of the Chinese policy of transforming the New Silk Road policy into a global phenomenon and an international strategy for peaceful cooperation and growth. The summit was attended by 29 foreign heads of state, government officials from more than 130 countries, 70 international organizations, and over a thousand delegates. Included among the attendees were the Chairwoman of the German Schiller Institute, Mrs. Helga Zepp-LaRouche, and other representatives of the Schiller Institute, including the two members who researched and authored this report.

In his opening speech, President Xi made the method and objectives of the BRI crystal clear.[5] Stressing the need for a new set of international relations to replace geopolitics, he said:

> First, we should build the Belt and Road into a road for peace. The ancient silk routes thrived in times of peace, but lost vigor in times of war. The pursuit of the Belt and Road Initiative requires a peaceful and stable environment. We should foster a new type of international relations featuring "win-win" cooperation; and we should forge partnerships of dialogue with no confrontation, and of friendship rather than alliance.

He also noted the importance of the principle of sovereignty and independence for nations that have suffered much in the past few decades due to unjustified military interventions by major powers: "All countries should respect each other's sovereignty, dignity and territorial integrity, each other's development paths and social systems, and each other's core interests and major concerns."

Concerning the essence of the Chinese concept of "sustainable development," Xi explained: "Industries are the foundation of economy. We should deepen industrial cooperation so that industrial development

---

4. See: http://www.beltandroadforum.org/english/index.html

5. Full text of the speech: http://news.xinhuanet.com/english/2017-05/14/c_136282982.htm

plans of different countries will complement and reinforce each other. Focus should be put on launching major projects. We should strengthen international cooperation on production capacity and equipment manufacturing.... Infrastructure connectivity is the foundation of development through cooperation. We should promote land, maritime, air and cyberspace connectivity, concentrate our efforts on key passageways, cities and projects, and connect networks of highways, railways and seaports."

China's Role in the Economic Renaissance of West Asia and Africa

The BRI is based on the solid foundation of China's own economic miracle in the past few decades. It has evolved from a national Chinese project of economic development and industrialization into a massive intercontinental initiative for connectivity and economic cooperation, an initiative that more than 60 nations have joined so far, and that can potentially become the biggest economic undertaking in the history of mankind. West Asia and Africa, which enjoy massive geographical advantages and human and natural resources, are poised to reap major benefits from this global initiative.

The fact that China is sharing its amazing experience of industrialization and development of the past three decades with the rest of the world is a key element of success. China lifted 600 million of its citizens out of poverty between 1981 and 2004—as attested by such institutions as the World Bank[6]—through investments in urban and rural infrastructure projects, and megaprojects in transportation, water and power. This is an unparalleled achievement that can be replicated in the Middle East and Africa. Within this 23-year period, China built more water management projects than the United States had done in a hundred years. Another amazing indication of this feat is that China used more

Xinhua/Chen Cheng

The first train of the Chinese-financed Mombasa-Nairobi Standard Gauge Railway (SGR) arrives at Nairobi Terminus in Nairobi, capital of Kenya, May 31, 2017.

cement in the three years 2011-2013, than did the United States during the entire 20th Century![7] China's 11,000 km high-speed railway network (which is planned to reach 20,000 km in the next decade), has already surpassed the combined network of the Western European nations. China has 37 operating nuclear power plants (70% of which were built in the past decade alone), and a further 20 plants are under construction.

Through the BRI, China is offering the rest of the world its know-how, experience and technology, backed by a $3 trillion financial arsenal. This is a great opportunity for West Asia and Africa to realize the dreams of the post-World War II independence era, dreams that have unfortunately been sabotaged for decades. The dramatic deficit in infrastructure both nationally and inter-regionally in West Asia and Africa can, ironically, be considered in this new light as a great opportunity. Although many other industrial nations in Europe, Asia and the Americas have technological and labor capabilities similar to those of China, they lack the vision and political will to apply these capabilities

---

6. See: http://www.worldbank.org/en/news/feature/2010/03/19/results-profile-china-poverty-reduction

7. https://www.washingtonpost.com/news/wonk/wp/2015/03/24/how-china-used-more-cement-in-3-years-than-the-u-s-did-in-the-entire-20th-century/?utm_term=.078c78e82bfb

and to finance their use. Since West Asia and Africa combined is such a strategically important area for both East and West, it is, therefore, a perfect place for bringing the capabilities of the nations of the world into one concrete project of peaceful cooperation and development.

Encouraging signs have simultaneously emerged from African nations that have realized the importance of joining and benefitting from the new paradigm of development based on industrialization and large-scale infrastructure projects. Egypt and Ethiopia, for example, have both designed impressive national development plans that are being implemented in rapid steps. But even here, especially in Ethiopia, China's role is decisive.

China's commitment and farsightedness in helping develop the economies of the African nations was eloquently expressed in President Xi Jinping's Dec 4, 2015 speech at the Summit of the Forum on China-Africa Cooperation (FOCAC) held in Johannesburg, South Africa.[8]

President Xi stated that "by the end of 2014, the total stock of Chinese investment in Africa had reached $101 billion, resulting in more than 3,100 Africa-based enterprises." He added that "two-way trade reached $221.9 billion in 2014," emphasizing that China "has become Africa's principal cooperation partner in such areas as trade, investment, infrastructural development and economic cooperation parks."

Referencing China's own experience in development and poverty alleviation, he said: "Industrialization is an inevitable path to a country's economic success. Within a short span of several decades, China has accomplished what took developed countries hundreds of years to accomplish and put in place a complete industrial system with an enormous production capacity."

Encouraging African leaders to pursue a path of industrialization, a call never heard from leaders of industrial nations in the West, President Xi stated: "It is en-

Xinhua/Jiang Xintong

A Chinese train driver teaches a local worker on Nigeria's first standard gauge railway, as part of capacity building for local railway personnel.

tirely possible for Africa, as the world's most promising region in terms of development potential, to bring into play its advantages and achieve great success.... The achievement of inclusive and sustainable development in Africa hinges on industrialization, which holds the key to creating jobs, eradicating poverty and improving people's living standards."

While emphasizing that Africa's path to industrialization should be found by Africans, he stressed that "It is China's sincere hope to share its experience with African countries, and we are willing to provide capital, technology and personnel in support of African industrialization."

Breaking with the idea of technological apartheid, President Xi declared that "China is ready to share, without any reservation, advanced applicable technology with Africa and to combine Chinese competitive industries with African needs for development to deepen industrial cooperation." He also promised to open vocational centers in Africa for training African personnel.

The outcome of the Johannesburg Summit was in harmony with President Xi's call. The final Declaration of the summit emphasized that the two sides—China and Africa—will promote the process of industrialization and agricultural modernization in Africa and focus on strengthening cooperation in infrastructure projects including, but not limited to, railways,

---

8. Text of the speech can be found here: http://www.focac.org/eng/ltda/dwjbzjjhys_1/zyjh/

highways, regional aviation, power, water supply, information and communication, airport and ports, as well as human resource development. The declaration also underscored the importance of integrating Africa into the BRI.[9]

Thus, the stage has been officially set for one of the greatest endeavors in human history.

What Is 'Win-Win' Philosophy?

According to Chinese official media sources,[10] President Hu Jintao was the first Chinese leader to use this term in a speech on China's cooperation with other Asian nations, which he delivered in the Boao Forum in 2004.[11] President Hu used it again during his visit to Seattle, Washington, in 2006, describing China's position that, "as long as China and the United States view and handle bilateral relations from a strategic height and long-term perspective, seize their common strategic interests, and enhance exchanges and cooperation with mutual respect and on an equal footing, they will realize the reciprocal and win-win results."

In April 2011, Foreign Minister of China Yang Jiechi delivered a speech titled "Win-Win Cooperation for Harmonious Development" at the opening ceremony of the Tenth "Spring of Diplomats" event in Beijing, in which he said: "China will unswervingly carry out the win-win strategy of opening-up. China cannot develop in isolation of the world, and China's development brings benefits to the world. China does not pursue its interests at the expense of other countries or seek to maximize its own interests. What we want is to expand the common interests with other countries and integrate our own interests with the common interests of the entire world with a view to achieving common development."

President Xi presented the most detailed and eloquent description of this notion in his speech at the General Debate of the 70th Session of the UN General Assembly in September 2015:[12]

"We should renew our commitment to the purposes and principles of the UN Charter, build a new type of international relations featuring win-win cooperation, and create a community of shared future for mankind," he said, stressing that to achieve this goal nations "should build partnerships in which countries treat each other as equals, engage in mutual consultation and show mutual understanding," and that "the principle of sovereign equality underpins the UN Charter.... The future of the world must be shaped by all countries. All countries are equals." President Xi further explained: "We should be committed to multilateralism and reject unilateralism. We should adopt a new vision of seeking win-win outcomes for all, and reject the outdated mindset that one's gain means the other's loss or that the winner shall take all. Consultation is an important form of democracy, and it should also become an important means of exercising contemporary international governance."

President Xi usually uses the description that programs of development proposed by China "will be open and inclusive, not exclusive. They will be a real chorus comprising all countries along the routes, not a solo for China itself."[13] The usual skepticism expressed in discussing China's intentions behind the BRI strategy is partly motivated by a sense of rivalry and fear by those who harbor the typical geopolitical notions inherited from centuries of imperialist rivalries, colonialism, and slavery. Ironically, these notions are also shared by the victims of these evils, who view every major power as an egoistic force whose only concern is to take, and never to give or to collaborate. On the other hand, a great deal of this skepticism is based on ignorance of China's culture and of its historical characteristics.

These two matters have been thoroughly addressed, not by a Chinese, but by a European personality with the most knowledge of, and personal involvement in this Chinese initiative in the Western world. That is Mrs. Helga Zepp-LaRouche, a German citizen, founder and chairwoman of the international Schiller Institute, and wife of American economist and statesman Lyndon LaRouche. Her 40-year involvement—in collaboration with her husband and associates in the Schiller Institute around the world—in defining the principles and propagating the importance of connecting all the continents of the globe through infrastructure and development

9. Text of the Johannesburg FOCAC Summit Declaration: http://www.focac.org/eng/ltda/dwjbzjjhys_1/hywj/t1327960.htm

10. Source: http://english.cntv.cn/2015/10/20/ARTI144532512 0332760.shtml

11. Text of the speech: http://english.gov.cn/archive/publications/2016/01/13/content_281475271412746.htm

12. The speech was titled "Working Together to Forge a New Partnership of Win-win Cooperation and Create a Community of Shared Future for Mankind." https://gadebate.un.org/sites/default/files/gastatements/70/70_ZH_en.pdf

13. Speech at the Boao Forum for Asia Annual Conference in March 2015: http://english.boaoforum.org/hynew/19353.jhtml

corridors, has gained her the nick-name "New Silk Road Lady" in Chinese media.

Mrs. Zepp-LaRouche thoroughly described the ideological problems facing Europeans when exploring the BRI in a speech she delivered in the Swedish capital, Stockholm, in January 2017.[14]

She explained that "the problem with Europe, is that the European Union bureaucracy and some governments, are still in the old paradigm, the geopolitical paradigm of globalization, of neoliberal policies." Zepp-LaRouche stressed that "most people, at least in Europe and in the United States, cannot imagine that governments are instituted to promote the common good, because we have not experienced that for such a long time. The common idea of all the think-tanks, or most think-tanks, is 'China must have ulterior motives' or 'China is just trying to replace Anglo-American imperialism, with a Chinese imperialism.'"[15]

Zepp-LaRouche stated that her extensive studies of China since her 1971 visit—as one of the first Western journalists to go to China in the middle of the Cultural Revolution—show that these claims are not true. "I have seen China as it was then; I traveled to Beijing, Tianjin, Qingdao, Shanghai, and to the countryside, and so I know what an enormous transformation China has made in this period," she said.

At a June 2015 international conference of the Schiller Institute in Paris, Zepp-LaRouche discussed

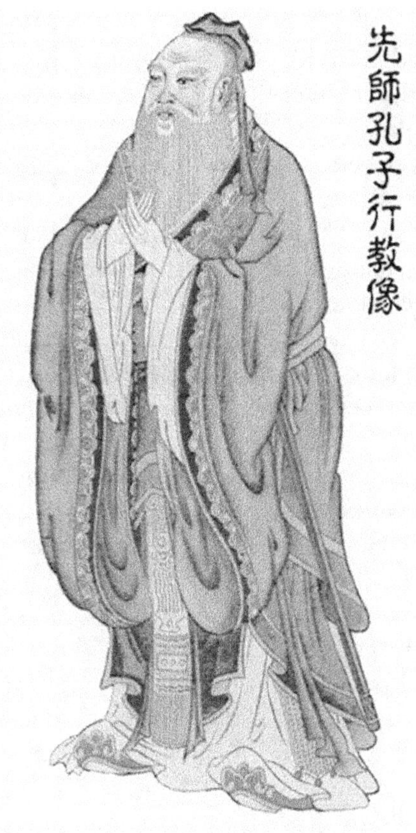

Confucius
BC 551-479

the core of the philosophy behind China's current win-win notion of its policies, and why that philosophy coheres perfectly with the true humanist Christian values of Europe. Here are some excerpts of her speech:[16]

Confucius (BC 551-479) has, along with Mencius (BC 372-289), influenced Chinese philosophy, actually the Chinese state philosophy, for about 2,500 years. That philosophy has an image of man that man is good by nature. The key notions of the Chinese philosophy are *ren,* which is the idea corresponding to "agapē"—love, charity in the Christian tradition; and the idea of *li,* meaning "principle," which is the idea that if each person and each thing develops in the best possible way, you have harmony in society. This corresponds to the idea of Cardinal Nicolas of Cusa (1401-1464), that if each microcosm develops in the best way, you have concordance in the macrocosm; or the idea of the monad of Leibniz, that if each develops his fullest potential, you have harmony.

Now, the idea of harmony is very central to Confucian philosophy. It is not an aesthetic relationship, but a contrapuntal development of mutual forward development: If all microcosms develop in the optimal way, you have harmony in the macrocosm.

There's also the idea that there is such a thing as the Mandate of Heaven: that there must be harmony between nature and man, and this comes originally from the idea of God's will of the Western Zhou dynasty, from BC 1046-771, which said that there must be harmony between

---

14. Full text of the speech: http://newparadigm.schillerinstitute.com/blog/2017/01/11/helga-zepp-larouche-lifts-stockholm-audience-sublime-schiller-instituteeir-seminar/

15. Typical of what Mrs. LaRouche is referring to here is a very widespread notion among many academics. See the book review titled "The Chinese Invade Africa" by Ian Johnson, *New York Review of Books,* September 25, 2014 (http://www.nybooks.com/articles/2014/09/25/chinese-invade-africa/) and see the BBC report titled "China follows British footsteps to African wealth" (http://news.bbc.co.uk/2/hi/programmes/from_our_own_correspondent/9023642.stm).

16. Full text: http://www.larouchepub.com/hzl/2015/4225paris_conf_jun13.html

the heavens and man, and that they are closely related.

Harmony without uniformity is what Confucius writes about in his *Analects*. Unity in diversity is the idea as expressed by Nicholas of Cusa. In the *Book of Rites*, which is the preface to the *Great Learning* of Confucius—it's attributed to him—he writes: "Now, harmony in society and among nations is based on an understanding of the principles of things." This is the same idea Friedrich Schiller (1789-1805) has in his *Letters Upon the Aesthetic Education of Man*, that only scientists and Classical artists understand the truth.

Xi Jinping, in his book, *Governance of China*, a collection of 71 of his speeches from 2013-14, reflects this Confucian spirit. He quotes an ancient Chinese saying: "Learning is the bow, while competence is the arrow. You should regard learning as the top priority, a responsibility, a moral support and a lifestyle. You should establish a conviction that dreams start from learning." He continued: "This is what Confucius meant when he said 'if you can in one day renovate yourself, do so from day to day.' Yes, let there be daily renovation. Life never favors those who follow the beaten track, and are satisfied with the status quo, and it never waits for the unambitious and those who sit idle and enjoy the fruits of others' work."

Therefore, this new model of cooperation among nations is not a utopia, but a vision of the future. The closest thinker in the European philosophical tradition to Confucius, Nicolas of Cusa, created an epochal new philosophical approach, which really separated the Middle Ages from modern times. He said the principle bringing about order and wholeness, the idea of concordance, of a universal concordance in the universe, is that harmony is not an aesthetic thing, but that in a contrapuntal way, the different microcosms must develop each other to the fullest, to the benefit of the other—the "win-win" idea; also the principle of the Peace of Westphalia (1648).

The Age of Mega-Projects Is Back

The negative paradigm shift that took off in the early 1970s in the United States and Europe, ushered in with the official takedown of the Franklin Roosevelt-era Bretton Woods system beginning under the Nixon Administration in August 1971, created a chain of financial and debt crises in the 1980s and 1990s around the globe. The focus shifted away from the state-financed industrial development policies that made possible the 1930s recovery from the Great Depression in the United States, and enabled Europe to recover from World War II. The new tendencies towards deregulation of financial and credit markets and towards globalization, made financial and monetary gains the primary criteria for investment. The creation of ever-greater financial bubbles and derivatives bubbles became the key element of financial practice, and public investment institutions and private resources moved gradually into the financial sector which promised ever greater profits on purely financial tools and products rather than physical economic development.

These neo-liberal policies found a suitable ally in the environmentalist movement, which was opposed to large-scale, modern industrial development, and the two worked hand in hand to prevent governments from financing large-scale infrastructure, industrial expansion, or scientific projects. The focus shifted simply to maintaining what was previously built and to building ever smaller projects. Developing nations became unable to receive credit and technologies from the industrialized sector to pursue their development goals, becoming more and more addicted to emergency aid and economic assistance programs. Instead of building dams, and water and sanitation systems, African nations were offered mosquito nets to fight disease, and were offered contraceptives to reduce birth rates, rather than help to build a modern health care system.

With the Chinese economic surge in the beginning of the new millennium, and the outbreak of the unprecedented financial and banking crisis in 2008, a wake-up call was issued. Although China's direct exposure to the crash was minimal, dramatically reduced trade with the declining economies of Europe and the United States affected China's economic growth. But unlike these trans-Atlantic nations, which resorted to more austerity measures and bank bail-out packages to the same financial institutions that created the crisis, China geared up its investments in infrastructure and industrial development as the way out of the crisis. The Chinese model became a source of inspiration for many other nations. However, while there is agreement on the importance of investment in large-scale infrastructure projects and growth in general to resolving the global financial and economic crisis, as was expressed by the G-20 Summit in Antalya, Turkey in November 2015,[17] the G-20 definition of "mega-projects," the technological level applied to them, and, most importantly, the ways of financing such large-scale infrastructure projects, differ greatly from the Chinese model. Additionally, many think-tanks and mass-media outlets continue to warn against investments in mega-projects—often defined by them as simply any project costing over $1 billion—for the reason that such projects are unlikely to generate a short-term monetary return. Some of the most-circulated criticisms of mega-projects do not really make any sense, since the authors of such criticism seem to say: "Well, sometimes governments mismanage large projects.... Therefore, we should never have any of them, ever!"[18]

As will be shown in the relevant sections of this report, investments in infrastructure create value far beyond any direct monetary profit to the investors. These investments are meant to raise the productivity of the individual and society as a whole, wherein the real wealth creation process lies. Mega-projects are transformative in nature, creating a great chain of developments. And they are technology generators, forcing the expansion of technological capabilities beyond current boundaries, as they pose new types of problems for society to solve—as seen in the fantastic advances made in achieving the goals of the U.S. Apollo space program in the 1960s.

The mega-projects that survived the economic downturn of the industrialized sector are singularities, remarkable for the general infrastructure void in which they have been completed. Such projects, completed against great financial odds and environmentalist resistance, are usually driven by necessity, such as solving traffic problems between regions, rather than as

NASA

Launch of Apollo 11, which put the first humans on the Moon.

part of a larger national and regional economic plan. Examples include the Vasco da Gama Bridge in Lisbon, Portugal (completed in 1998), the Øresund Bridge/Tunnel between Denmark and Sweden (completed in 1999), the "Big Dig" Central Artery Tunnel Project in Boston, USA (1991-2007), the Incheon Bridge in South Korea (completed 2009), Spain's national high-speed railway network (built 1992-2016), and the Gotthard Base Tunnel in the Swiss Alps (completed in 2016).

Otherwise, when it comes to the past two decades, China tops the list of such projects and is contributing to similar projects abroad. However, such overseas infrastructure projects invested in by China are part of a larger development process, not objects in and of themselves. This has to be taken in consideration when planning the development of West Asia and Africa, as will be explained in the chapters of this report.

---

17. Source: http://www.consilium.europa.eu/en/press/press-releases/2015/11/16-g20-summit-antalya-communique/. See also the joint World Bank-IMF report, "From Billions to Trillions: Transforming Development Finance": http://siteresources.worldbank.org/DEVCOM-MINT/Documentation/23659446/DC2015-0002%28E%29Financingf orDevelopment.pdf

18. See, for example, this report from the U.S. Cato Institute: https://www.cato.org/policy-report/januaryfebruary-2017/megaprojects-over-budget-over-time-over-over, or this newspaper article in the Canadian *Globe and Mail:* https://www.theglobeandmail.com/opinion/move-over-megaprojects-here-come-the-teraprojects/article27973165/

Redefining 'Sustainable Development'

The term "sustainable development" was formally codified by the United Nations through the 1987 Brundtland Report.[19] It is usually associated with promoting the use of so-called "renewable" sources of energy, such as solar and wind, and is generally coupled with a concern over alleged adverse impacts of human activity on the environment. The referenced Brundtland report states that "sustainable development" is defined as sufficient development to cover the "basic needs" of poor societies, i.e., the bare minimum to ensure survival, while also arguing that all nations and peoples have the right to fulfill their aspirations for better living standards. However, it states that most people in modern societies "live beyond the world's ecological means, for instance in our patterns of energy use," leading to its conclusion that the world is doomed to poverty; technological progress and industrial development are not real solutions, because sustainable development implies "the idea of limitations imposed by the state of technology and social organization on the environment's ability to meet present and future needs."

As will be shown in Chapter 3, the notions of "limited natural resources" and the so-called "carrying capacity of the ecological system" are not applicable to human society, since it is the level of scientific and technological progress which defines the range of "resources," rather than an *a priori* "natural" limit. Therefore, adopting the "sustainable development" goals determined by such notions as in the Brundtland Report poses a great obstacle to eliminating poverty and providing higher living standards and quality of life for all individuals and nations. We need a new definition of these notions, or completely different concepts.

China has proven that the way out of poverty and onto the path of progress is through fast-track "industrialization" and large-scale development projects and mega-projects, using the full range of resources, whether scientific, human, or natural. For example, all useful sources of energy, such as coal, oil and gas, hydropower and nuclear power must be used. While it is imperative that the sources of power with a greater energy-flux density, like nuclear fission and fusion, should replace the less dense sources, it is neither reasonable nor moral to ask poor nations to avoid the sources of power that enabled the United States, Europe, Japan and others to become modern industrial societies.

China's economic miracle is based on implementing sound policies that seem to be the opposite of those demanded by such international institutions as the World Bank, the IMF, international environmental organizations, and financial consulting corporations and think tanks. China has followed a policy which was, ironically, the policy that made the U.S. the greatest economic power on earth by the end of the 1940s, and made a ruined Germany the second greatest industrial power in the post-World War II world.

China's is a dirigist policy of centralized, state-financed development of infrastructure and industry through national credits for long-term development, by using the latest technological and scientific innovations and developing new ones. Nowhere in China's policies do we find the internationally much-touted public-private partnership (PPP), or wholesale privatization of state assets; the decentralization of economic policy making; or the mixing of commercial banking activities with speculative investment banking. Nonetheless, Western institutions keep insisting that the developing sector nations should commit to privatization, decentralization, the PPP mode of financing, and a reduction in the involvement of the state in economic planning and execution of policies.[20]

This discrepancy—between the proven, successful methods of development, both current and historical (as in industrialization of the United States and Germany, for example) on the one hand, and what is being promoted by international institutions on the other—must be cleared out and eliminated. The new paradigm of development spearheaded by China and the BRICS nations is a key element in this process.

It is therefore necessary to state in clear terms here, in this context, that the definition of the term "sustain-

---

19. Former Norwegian Prime Minister Gro Harlem Brundtland headed the UN-appointed World Commission on Environment and Development, releasing the report "Our Common Future," also known as the Brundtland Report, in 1987: http://www.un-documents.net/wced-ocf.htm

20. Source referenced above: joint World Bank-IMF report "From Billions to Trillions: Transforming Development Finance" (http://siteresources.worldbank.org/DEVCOMMINT/Documentation/23659446/DC2015-0002%28E%29FinancingforDevelopment.pdf) and Antaliya G-20 Summit Communiqué (http://www.consilium.europa.eu/en/press/press-releases/2015/11/16-g20-summit-antalya-communique/).

able development" should mean the ability to "maintain" a process of providing ever higher standards of living, both physically and culturally, to whole societies through scientific creativity and technological innovation. "Sustainable development" should not be used to mean the adaptation by society to an ever-shrinking base of fixed resources, because there is no such a thing as limited resources! What puts a limit to growth is the lack of cultural, scientific and technological progress.

A better term to describe this evolutionary process is "progress" or "progressive development."

'Helping' or Empowering Africa?

One the biggest obstacles in the way of establishing equitable partnerships between Africa on the one hand and Europe and the United States on the other, is that, while in the colonial period Africa was considered a mere looting ground, in the post-colonial era, Africa continued to be considered as a source of raw materials, but was also increasingly regarded as a burden that could only be helped by "relief" and "foreign aid" rather than cooperation to build the means by which African nations could become self-reliant to meet their economic and social needs. Where Europe and the United States see only problems, China sees potentials and opportunities.

Such positive thinking is not limited to China. U.S. President Franklin Delano Roosevelt (FDR) had a similar view of Africa. FDR—who rescued the U.S. economy after the Great Depression hit, and helped rid the world of Fascism and Nazism during World War II through using U.S. industrial and logistical capabilities during his New Deal economic revival years in the 1930s—held very strong anti-colonial sentiments and views. His heated encounters with British Prime Minister Winston Churchill, documented by his son Elliott Roosevelt, a U.S. Air Force officer who at times accompanied his father to international conferences during the war,[21] attest to his vision of what should have happened after the war. Unfortunately, FDR died before the war ended, and his successors did not follow up on his

President Franklin D. Roosevelt and the British Empire's Prime Minister, Winston Churchill, in Casablanca, Jan. 22, 1943.

progressive views and policies.

Two excerpts from exchanges between FDR and Churchill show the extent of the difference between their two perspectives:[22]

> Churchill shifted in his armchair. "The British Empire trade agreements" he began heavily, "are—"
>
> Father broke in. "Yes. Those Empire trade agreements are a case in point. It's because of them that the people of India and Africa, of all the colonial Near East and Far East, are still as backward as they are."
>
> Churchill's neck reddened and he crouched forward. "Mr. President, England does not propose for a moment to lose its favored position among the British Dominions. The trade that has made England great shall continue, and under conditions prescribed by England's ministers."
>
> "You see," said Father slowly, "it is along in here somewhere that there is likely to be some disagreement between you, Winston, and me.
>
> "I am firmly of the belief that if we are to arrive at a stable peace it must involve the development of backward countries. Backward peo-

---

21. Elliott Roosevelt, *As He Saw It*, 1946.

22. *Ibid.*

Senegalese scholar and scientist Cheikh Anta Diop in 1960 called for industrialization, nuclear power, and the highest levels of education.

ples. How can this be done? It can't be done, obviously, by eighteenth-century methods. Now—"

"Who's talking eighteenth-century methods?"

"Whichever of your ministers recommends a policy which takes wealth in raw materials out of a colonial country, but which returns nothing to the people of that country in consideration. Twentieth-century methods involve bringing industry to these colonies. Twentieth-century methods include increasing the wealth of a people by increasing their standard of living, by educating them, by bringing them sanitation— by making sure that they get a return for the raw wealth of their community."

Elsewhere in the book, Roosevelt told Churchill:

"Wealth! Imperialists don't realize what they can do, what they can create! They've robbed this continent of billions, and all because they were too short-sighted to understand that their billions were pennies, compared to the possibilities! Possibilities that must include a better life for the people who inhabit this land …"

The African Union Aims High

A new vision of the future emerged in Africa most dramatically in 2014, after a crucial period of preparation. In January 2014, Nkosazana Dlamini-Zuma, the Chairperson of the African Union Commission (AUC), published what could be called the new, or second vision and manifesto for African industrialization and integration, her "Email from the Future."

There had been no such African document since Senegal's Cheikh Anta Diop, in 1960, published his passionate vision of creating "a powerful State industry, giving primacy to industrialization, development, and mechanization of agriculture," with nuclear power production and technical institutes in such fields as nuclear physics and chemistry, electronics, and aeronautics (see Chapter 9).

Dlamini-Zuma released her impassioned vision on the occasion of the January 2014 ministerial retreat of the African Union (AU) Executive Council. It takes the form of a personal letter from "Nkosazana" to a friend named "Kwame," written in 2063—the 100th anniversary of the founding of the AU's precursor, the Organization of African Unity.[23] In her wide-ranging letter, the building up and integration of African infrastructure are prominent. Looking back from 2063, she wrote, for example:

> Economic integration, coupled with infrastructure development, saw intra-Africa trade mushrooming, from less than 12% in 2013 to almost 50% by 2045. This integration was further consolidated with the growth of commodity exchanges and continental commercial giants. Starting with the African pharmaceutical company, Pan African companies now not only dominate our domestic market of over two billion people, but they have overtaken multi-nationals from the rest of the world in their own markets.
>
> Even more significant than this, was the growth of regional manufacturing hubs, around the beneficiation of our minerals and natural resources, such as in the Eastern Congo, North-Eastern Angola and Zambia's copper belt and at major Silicon valleys in Kigali, Alexandria, Brazzaville, Maseru, Lagos and Mombasa, to mention but a few such hubs.

23. "Agenda 2063: an e-mail from the future," Dr. Nkosazana Dlamini-Zuma, AU publication, 2014.

African Union Commission Chair Dr. Nkosazana Dlamini-Zuma, Oct. 24, 2016.

Kunene, Limpopo and many others—financed by Public Private Partnerships (PPPs) that involved African and BRIC investors, as well as the African Diaspora, released the continent's untapped agricultural potential. …"

… [T]he African Express Rail now connects all the capitals of our former states, and indeed they will be able to crisscross and see the beauty, culture and diversity of this cradle of humankind. The marvel of the African Express Rail is that it is not only a high-speed train, with adjacent highways, but also contains pipelines for gas, oil, and water, as well as ICT broadband cables: African ownership, integrated planning and execution at its best!

My friend, Africa has indeed transformed herself from an exporter of raw materials with a declining manufacturing sector in 2013, to become a major food exporter, a global manufacturing hub, a knowledge centre, beneficiating our natural resources and agricultural products as drivers to industrialization. Pan African companies, from mining to finance, food and beverages, hospitality and tourism, pharmaceuticals, fashion, fisheries and ICT are driving integration, and are amongst the global leaders in their sectors.

We are now the third largest economy in the world. As the Foreign Ministers' retreat in Bahir Dar in January 2014 emphasized, we did this by finding the balance between market forces and strong and accountable developmental states and Regional Economic Communities (RECs) to drive infrastructure, the provision of social services, industrialization and economic integration.

Let me recall what our mutual friend recently wrote:

"The (African) agrarian revolution had small beginnings. Successful business persons (and local governments) with roots in the rural areas started massive irrigation schemes to harness the waters of the continent's huge river systems. The pan-African river projects—on the Congo, the Nile, Niger, Gambia, Zambezi,

A flagship project of this vision, the African Express Rail, renamed the African Integrated High Speed Railway Network (AIHSRN) project, was initiated six months later at the AU Summit by the AU Executive Council.

The context of this exciting development is to be found both in Africa and China. Dlamini-Zuma had become chairperson of the AUC in 2012 and, having been South Africa's foreign minister from 1999 to 2009, she already had strong ideas about what direction Africa should take. Xi Jinping had become President of China in 2012 and had already developed his concept for a New Silk Road. When Dlamini-Zuma and Xi met in Beijing in February 2013, it was a meeting of two minds.

In May 2013, the vision whose formulation she was leading, called Agenda 2063, was discussed by the AU Assembly of Heads of State and Government (AU-AHSG). Her "Email from the Future" followed in January 2014. In May 2014, Li Keqiang, Premier of China, visited the AUC in Addis Ababa as part of a broader tour of Africa, and pledged "cooperation between Africa and China in high-speed railway, aviation, highways, and industrialization infrastructure," and included in that cooperation the project to connect all African capital cities with high-speed rail.

After the Agenda 2063 Framework Document was adopted in September 2015 by the AU-AHSG, Dlamini-Zuma, at the invitation of Foreign Minister Wang Yi, went to Beijing in November for a six-day visit, to take Africa-China cooperation forward. She rode on the Beijing-Tianjin high-speed train for the first time, accompanied by Ambassador Kuang Weiling, the head of the new, permanent mission of China to the AU, established at AU request. Her ride on a high-speed train was symbolic of one of the underlying principles of Agenda 2063, that Africa must proceed by leap-frogging to the most advanced solutions and the most advanced technologies.

Africa Must Leap Ahead, Not Crawl Forward!

Some in the West say that African development should be through "appropriate technologies," that an incremental approach to improvement should be taken, that foot-powered treadle pumps for water, or solar panels on huts would be a useful upgrade. This outlook must be rejected.

Chinese-financed and -built Soubre hydroelectric power station near the city of Soubre in Cote d'Ivoire initiated electricity generation, July 1, 2017.

Instead, Africa should have the best and latest technologies, and the greatest ambitions not only to pull its peoples out of poverty and underdevelopment, but to move them to a completely new economic platform. The Congo River, for example, could support the production of an estimated 100 GW of hydroelectricity, enough for hundreds of millions of people, with 40 GW from the planned Grand Inga Dam alone. The Transaqua water transfer program—which would use a small fraction of the water from the Congo and its tributaries to refill Lake Chad, provide a navigation means in Central Africa, and generate great amounts of hydropower—would be larger by an order of magnitude than any other water project in the world (see Chapter 6, Transaqua: The Centerpiece of African Development).

The expansion of rail lines in Africa is currently at a world-leading level. New transportation routes across Africa will connect the hinterlands to the cities and ports, allowing modern development. With access to efficient transportation, regions benefit from opportunities to bring in equipment and supplies, to export their products, and for residents to travel. With the availability of electricity, higher productive capabilities are unlocked, and the value of the land and the people increases.

Incredible potential for growth exists in Africa and West Asia! This report will explain projects that are proposed and those underway, make proposals for a new level of connectivity and economic infrastructure for the region, and discuss the economic outlook and financing required to bring these programs to life.

However, before any proverbial shovels dig into the ground, a complete intellectual review is required to clear and overturn some dangerously false but generally accepted axioms and postulates regarding the human species' relationship to and its role in nature, what "resources" are, how societies develop, how development is financed, and the proper role for industrialized nations in West Asia and Africa. There are many such axioms and concepts that are treated almost as law or divine revelation, but they have been partially responsible for Africa's current state of poverty and lack of development, and they form a great obstacle to reversing these conditions. These will be dealt with in Chapters 3, 4 and 5.

Toward a Second Treaty of Westphalia: The Coming Eurasian World

by Lyndon H. LaRouche, Jr.

First, let us speak of tragedy.

Let such caricatures of poor King Canute as President George W. Bush, Jr., howl their denials, while they can still be heard. Let him shriek in futile rage against those thunderous winds of chaos which were already hurling themselves against the increasingly bankrupt national financial systems of the world. That chaos, now excited to the greater turbulence caused by the desperate antics of such poor, enraged fools as he, now descends with its own, added, uncontrollable fury upon our hapless, present world monetary-financial system. So, now, just a few weeks following our modern Canute's recent claims of electoral victory, the oncoming waves of a great storm of global breakdown crisis are striking on the gates of the governments of the world, and are already pounding the hoaxster's illusion of Bush's economic recovery to shreds. The terminal breakdown-crisis of the 1971-2004 world monetary system is thus now fully under way.

In that Classical definition of tragedy which takes its origin from ancient Greece, but contrary to the incompetent, Romantic doctrines usually taught in university courses on the subject of drama, a tragedy does not represent a calamity whose primary cause is an error by the current leadership of a society. Rather, *both the selection of, and the relevant failures by that leadership are determined by the systemic features of the culture and institutions within which both that selection of leadership, and the forces acting upon its behavior are operating.* Such is the U.S. situation today.[1]

White House/Eric Draper

"Like fabled King Canute," writes LaRouche, "U.S. President George W. Bush, Jr., has more the character of a piece of noxious flotsam floating on the flood waters of doom, than the true cause of the crisis in which he plays the part of the official First Fool."

subject, fall into the category of what I have described, pedagogically, as "fishbowl" syndromes, in which the leading figures of a tragedy are controlled by a system of belief inhering in that culture at that time. In such a systemic crisis, the need is for a leader who acts in a kind of defiance of the prevalent culture of his, or her society at that time, an efficient defiance which breaks the mold of tragedy, as President Franklin Roosevelt did when he replaced the tragic figure of President Herbert Hoover. In the typical tragedy, the failed leader has given into the culture's influence on him; it is that culture itself, combined with his want of the capacity to defy that culture's built-in imperatives, which is the culprit. Shakespeare's Hamlet and Schiller's Don Carlos and Wallenstein are examples of this, Schiller's for reason of the historical depth of his compositions. Romantics and their doctrines, of course, reject this, and seek the fault in the leader as such, rather than the culture which he represents all too well. Thus, the fact that President George W. Bush, Jr. is a virtual puppet of the cultural current he represents, is his fault. *The failure of the people and related institutions of the U.S. to ensure the selection of a qualified candidate, rather than this President, is the tragedy.*

---

1. Poor or bad quality of leadership does play a role, of course. However, systemic crises of the quality which a Classical tragedy takes as its

Look at the folly of the Peloponnesian war, and learn. As Plato understood, and showed in his dialogues, this was not the mistake of a leader, but of the way in which the behavior of leadership, from Pericles through Thrasymachus, and the Sophists of the Democratic Party of Athens, was governed by the ruling moral degeneracy permeating the leading institutions of the population of Athens during that span of decades. So, it is with the tragic forces which have controlled the step-by-step descent of the U.S.A. and western and central Europe into self-inflicted doom over, especially, the recent four decades. The people whose institutions arranged the selection of the nation's leaders, prefer to blame the leaders, as Romantics do, for the ills of society; they evade the question: Why they did prefer not to choose, or to develop better ones?

So, in the current case of the Bush Administration, the origin of the present crisis is less a product of that Administration, than those U.S.A. institutional forces, including the Democratic Party as much as the Republican, which have shaped the selection and behavior of the leadership and policies and practices of both government and also private institutions during a more immediate period of four decades. Much of the blame for this dates from wrongheaded changes in direction of U.S. policy-making outlook already under way since the regrettable selection of Senator Harry S Truman as a Democratic Party Vice-Presidential candidate in the Summer of 1944.

In an existential crisis, such as the present world situation, which has those or similar attributes of a threatened general breakdown of the system, the danger comes chiefly from the leadership which fails to break with the pre-established policy-shaping trends, the failure to break in the way President Franklin Roosevelt did in his 1932 election-campaign, and in the turnabout in U.S. policy which he introduced beginning his first hours in the Administration. Like fabled King Canute, U.S. President George W. Bush, Jr., has more the character of a piece of noxious flotsam floating on the flood waters of doom, than the true cause of the crisis in which he plays the part of the official First Fool.

The great leader for a time of crisis is one *whose selection* breaks the rules, those rotten rules which are the relevant expression of the relevant, essential corruption. For that reason, society has tolerated only a relatively few truly great leaders for more than a short time. For example, as in the case of President Charles de Gaulle of France's Fifth Republic after 1963, the way in which bad governments recur or are maintained, is that the relevant leading institutions of society kill or otherwise eliminate capable leaders, even one such as de Gaulle who saved his nation in a time of existential crisis, when his rivals could not; but, who go against the whims of the representatives of the currently leading body of opinion, and are then, first undermined, and, later, ousted by aid of a corrupted majority of popular opinion. As Solon of Athens wrote, such expressions of popular opinion are the true root of Classical tragedy.

It is a virtual rule, that a corrupt popular opinion turns quickly against the leader who rescues that people from the consequences of its own popular follies. So, the French ingratitude to de Gaulle might remind one of a celebrated apostle of France's Nineteenth-Century decadence, who wrote insightfully of the beggar, who attacked savagely the first person who offered the beggar alms.

Traditionally fickle, so-called "democratic" popular opinion sometimes treats the wrong-doers of its nation almost as savagely as it might express ingratitude toward its heroes. In this present state of crisis, nothing that the Bush Administration might have thought were to be its triumphant schemes for the months ahead, will go as planned. Anyone who assumes that Bush's intentions will be carried out as planned, is as much a fool as the doomed Bush himself.

It is typical of that paragon of gutter hypocrisy, Bush, that he is mobilizing now for what he solemnly swore, repeatedly, during the recent televised campaign debates, that he would never do, "privatize Social Security." He is as evil and stupid as a Gila monster, as he moves to reward the poor dupes who voted for him, by sadistically increasing the proportionate tax burdens on those poor, and looting their small pensions, while gleefully cutting the taxes on his friends, the rich, especially the legendary "filthy rich" of such as Enron and Halliburton notoriety.

That folly of his Administration will generate countervailing consequences, probably even the fools' uncalculated ones, like those which soon embraced the five great fools of 1914, the German Kaiser, the Austrian Kaiser, the Russian Czar, and the chauvinism of the British and French populations. So, the spirit of the plagues of ancient Egypt is already descending upon its lawful prey, that modern gutter-Pharaoh's realm.

Nonetheless, in this stormy moment, nothing is settled, except the fact that the greatest monetary-financial crisis in modern history is already buffeting the world.

French President Charles de Gaulle (left) with German Chancellor Konrad Adenauer, in 1961. De Gaulle, like all great leaders in a time of crisis, broke the rules in order to save his nation. He was later ousted by a corrupted majority of popular opinion.

In one way or another, this crisis is already threatening the Bush Administration with an early, self-inflicted doom. Meanwhile, what the actual outcome of this rising tumult might be, remains to be decided: by us, if we can find the will to do so.

Look at what faces the U.S. population in particular.

The Prospect Before You

This storm does not mean that this assault on the rulers of the system by the fabulous *Erinyes*, is necessarily aimed intentionally at you personally. Nor is this crisis of our contemporary planetary civilization, necessarily a final one. At least for this moment, the hatred which this Bush Administration has harvested from around the world, during the just less than four years of its reign, has destroyed that great political capital which our republic had once enjoyed in many parts of the world. In this and kindred ways, the regime of this petty, lunatic, and madly wicked tyrant, Bush, like that of England's Richard III, or the Emperor Nero before him, has crafted the instrument of cruelty which could turn about to destroy his reign.

Nonetheless, today, amid this mounting tumult, there are still some remaining options for rescuing civilization—and, for you too; but, only on the condition that we accept, quickly, the reality that we could not save both civilization and also that succubus which is the presently collapsing, liberals' monetary-financial system.

So, a system which has dominated the world's monetary-financial affairs since February 1763, that Anglo-Dutch Liberal model of monetary-financial system which created the present U.S. Bush regime, has reached the point of its own extreme decay. And we of the U.S.A. are presently trapped within the British (i.e., Anglo-Dutch Liberal imperialist) cultural vessel on which we have booked this forty-year journey toward Hell. This forty-year process has now reached the point, that neither that system, nor anything resembling it, could be saved, on either side of the Atlantic. It is as if sheeted Adam Smith, with lantern and spade, is walking toward the potter's field where his spiritual remains will be buried, soon, by the action of his own invisible hand. The rest of us, unfortunately, have already reached the stage at which the options for beginning to save our civilization will be diminishing rapidly, unless we begin to make, now, the relevant, drastic reforms we should have made decades ago.

It need not have turned out for us so badly as it has happened so far.

Had the victory of U.S. Democratic Presidential candidate John Kerry been announced on November 3, 2004, crucial discussions on the subject of this onrushing crisis would have begun between Senator Kerry's representatives and relevant figures of leading Eurasian nations. The mere fact, that such discussions were occurring, would have encouraged governments to adopt stop-gap measures which would minimize the risk, pending the coming U.S. January Presidential inauguration. Now, the incumbent Bush Administration's hysterical determination to proceed with new economic and related measures, measures more insane than those it had already introduced prior to November 2nd, creates a situation in which what had been the pending collapse of the system has now been triggered, and much worse is coming on, at an accelerating rate.

Indeed, Kerry could have had a clear victory in this election, had his Democratic Party not spent the months leading up to the Labor Day holiday doing as much as might be conceivable to throw the victory away before the campaign actually began. It was the same tragic cultural outlook of the Democratic Party organization which had already thrown away the 2000 Presidential election, which cheated the Party of the opportunity for a clear victory in November 2004. Having tasted the reputation for the apparent fresh defeat, the yet-to-be-redeemed elements of the Party often cover up for their own past errors by taking the view that the blame for the reported outcome was simply that the result had been inevitable, in any case, all along. They are saying, in effect: "Let's go back to those traditional ways" in which they lost election after Federal election, since the Great Gingrich Raid of November 1994. That pattern of resistance to needed change in outlook, is the systemic stuff of tragedy.

There are solutions; but, do not deceive yourself into imagining that I am proposing that we could simply turn back the clock to the better times of European civilization's earlier decades as easily as simply reversing the relevant worst policy-decisions of the recent four decades. You can not relight the candle you have just burned up. It is time for some of us to come together to address the new kinds of deeper challenges facing us now in our future, as not only a nation, but as a world civilization. We must assemble quickly, to study the coincidence of this crisis with other, onrushing changes which also have the character of planet-wide social-political upheavals of tectonic implications.

With the present systemic breakdown of that imperial, Anglo-Dutch Liberal system of finance which has dominated the planet increasingly since the February 10, 1763 Treaty of Paris, only an appropriate new system, replacing that Liberal system, could prevent the rapid descent of the planet as a whole into a new dark age. Therefore, we must now quickly craft and adopt a new system of relations among all of the leading sovereign nation-states of this planet, a treaty coherent with the principles of the 1648 peace Treaty of Westphalia. This requires a fresh view of the relations between peoples of, respectively, European and Asian cultures. Responsible people must now push forward, urgently, with the discussions needed to define the outlines of the needed direction of agreements.

In my writings on related matters, as published internationally over decades, I have presented the rudiments of those needed changes which are required, specifically, by Europe and the Americas. Those proposed remedies remain valid as the most appropriate model for the situation confronting those parts of the world today. However, there is also a still larger, problematic aspect to the present situation, an aspect beyond the confines of European tradition as usually defined. That is the aspect which I now address: the required, emerging new quality of relationships among the cultures of European and Asian origins.

One of the subjects which should occupy a leading place on that agenda, is the matter of the new long-term trends which have recently come to prominence, respecting the pressures for profound changes in the relationship between what had been defined by that relatively hegemonic role of that modern European culture, which emerged from the Italy-centered Fifteenth-Century Renaissance, on the one side, and, on the other side, the recent, seemingly explosive rise of the population of the nations of South and East Asia, as also Africa. [See **Figure 1**.] That is the purpose of this report.

In the following pages, I shall now proceed by, first, defining the concept of culture as this applies to the form of globally extended European civilization which began in ancient Greece. Then, second, proceeding from the basis of the matters of principle treated in the first of the following sections of this report, I shall argue the case for an equitable global treaty arrangement among both nations based upon European civilization and the Asian and other cultures which represent the remaining cultures of the planet.

1. Culture Unfolds in Long Waves

The shared function of the author, director, and players of a Classical tragedy, is to bring on stage the essential feature of either a part of a specific time and place in actual history, or a legendary past: to bring it on the stage in such a fashion that the member of the audience, seated perhaps in the balcony of that theater, relives that actual history, as a personal experience within his, or her own mind. The member of the audience must be assisted, but also challenged into putting himself, or herself, amid, even above, the highest level of the crucial decision-making of the actual, historically determined cultural realities of that recreated time and place. That member of the audience must get inside both the actually leading historical figures of that drama, and the culture of that time and place as well. That experience, so awakened within the tissues of the living mind of the individual member of the audience, is the transformation of an ordinary citizen, come in from the streets, into an impassioned statesman of that moment.

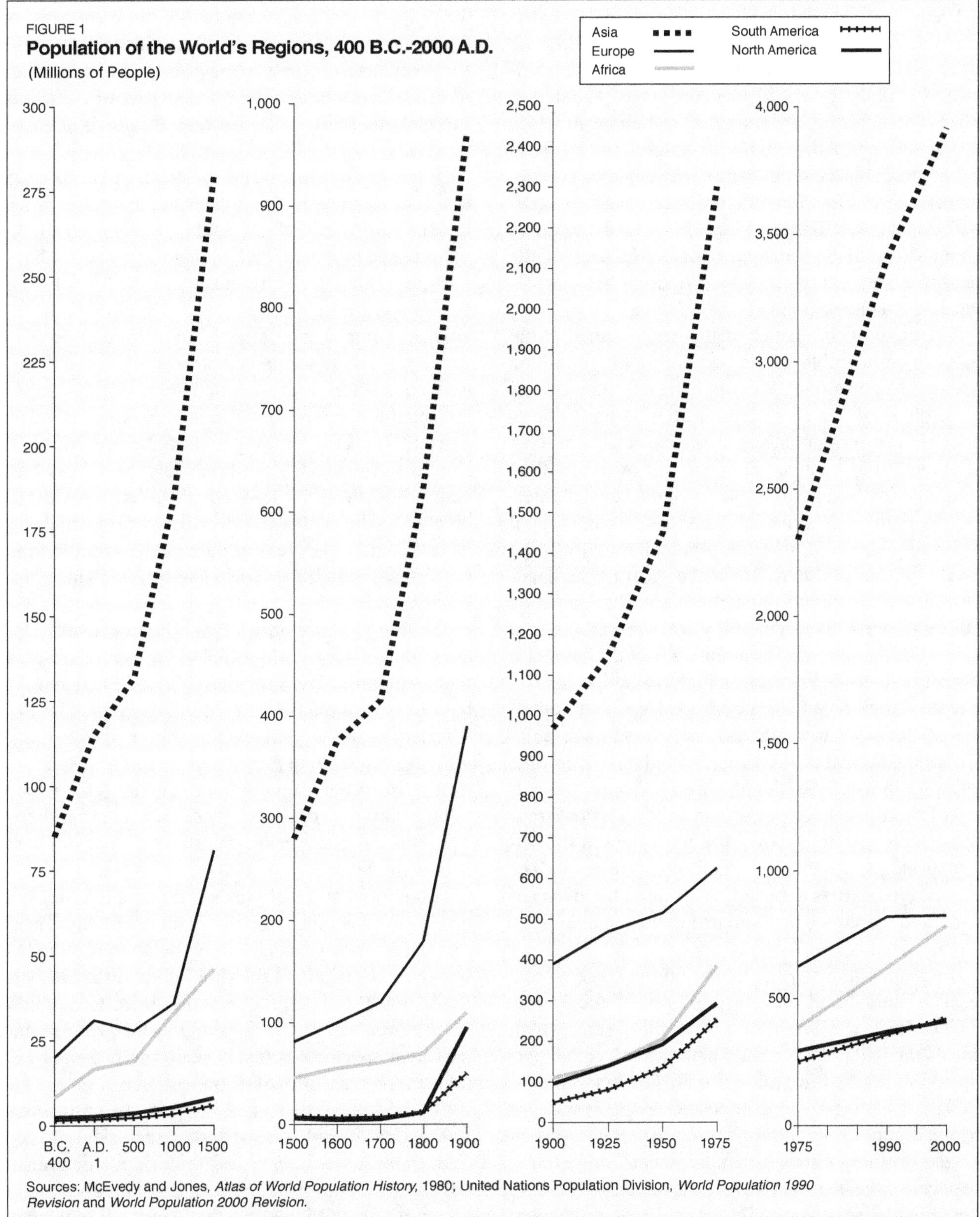

While always smaller than Asia in total population, European civilization displayed stronger increases in potential population density during the Renaissance and Industrial Revolution epochs, shown in the first two sections of the graph. The more recent generations show "profound changes in the relationship between what had been defined by that relatively hegemonic role of that modern European culture, which emerged from the Italy-centered Fifteenth-century Renaissance, on the one side, and, on the other side, the recent, seemingly explosive rise of the population of the nations of South and East Asia, as also Africa," LaRouche writes.

A great Classical tragedy is composed, and performed as a Platonic dialogue, such that the audience for that performance is placed, as in the intellectual balcony, overlooking that history on stage. From that higher vantage-point, the audience is challenged to see the interactions of the figures on stage from a higher vantage-point than virtually any of the depicted characters themselves. This Platonic requirement of the composition and performance of Classical tragedy, as noted by Plato himself on the subject of the failures of the tragedians, corresponds to what Friedrich Schiller defined as the vantage-point of *The Sublime*.

That view of the matter of the performance in the theater is comparable to the position of the qualified management consultant, for whom the interplay among the members of the client organization is the subject-matter of the professional's concern. He or she observes and judges from a higher standpoint of overview than any among the principals or others of the subject enterprise. As in my own personal experience of that fact, it was usually the case, that the problem actually to be solved was the problem which the existing management was certain did not exist; the client management's inability to solve the problem by its own independent means, was that its own behavior was not the subject it was inclined to address from a higher standpoint. The success of the consultation depended upon the clientele's willingness to adopt that higher vantage-point from which, then, it could recognize and thus overcome the failing in itself. So, the idealized patron in the balcony of the theater for performance of Classical tragedy, is challenged to discover the equivalent of the scientific principle which accounts for the failure of all of the combined parties depicted on stage, as by means of the method employed by Plato in composing a Socratic dialogue. That is *The Sublime*.

The players portray the action on the stage of real life. The author and players must reveal the *system* which controls the unfolding action, the system which controls the parts played, but which the individual participant in the real-life experience fails to recognize.

Classical tragedy, so composed, so performed, is thus the model for imparting a true sense for history in both the ordinary citizens, or adolescents, and others. The pages of the historian's book, the historian's lecture before the audience, must aim for, and accomplish that same effect: to bring the essence of real history, in the time and place it actually occurred, back into life within the mind of the audience, and of the historian, too.

Such Classical drama, so composed and delivered, is the properly mandatory foundation for the education of all of the actually qualified future citizens of a republic.

So, that said, now assume a seat in the amphitheater of Classical Athens. The second part of Aeschylus's Prometheus Trilogy, **Prometheus Bound**, is about to go on stage.

Since the morning after the death of U.S. President Franklin Roosevelt, this planet had been living in the kind of world-order that President neither intended, nor would have tolerated, had he lived to prevent what was set into motion under his successor. As his role behind the 1944 crafting of the post-war Bretton Woods, fixed-exchange-rate system attests, that President Roosevelt acted as a true statesman must, with a view of the long-term consequences of even short-term policy-decisions. He acted according to a specifically American way of patriotic thinking harking back to the precedent of his ancestor, Alexander Hamilton's ally, New York banker Isaac Roosevelt. Roosevelt intended the kinds of changes in the post-war order of the world which would have avoided the greatest part of the specific kind of willful evil which the world has suffered since his untimely death.

In the background of Franklin Roosevelt's Presidency, against the background of the funeral procession that saddening day, hear the voice of President Abraham Lincoln's Gettysburg Address, and then, in Ford's Theater, hear the shot by the traitor and enemy spy which brought about President Lincoln's most untimely death. Weep then, quietly and solemnly, for what our people have suffered on those accounts, still today. Think of the grave destiny with which our civilization is now threatened, now today.

Look now at Aeschylus's Prometheus Trilogy, as it could have been performed in an untaintedly Classical mode just a few years before his death (circa 456 B.C.), which is to say, about the time of the birth of Socrates (circa 469 B.C.) and a generation prior to the birth of Plato (circa 427 B.C.). Looking at that view from the past as a spectator actually seated in a theater of the present, see the following connections.

In the known history of the past, as, unfortunately, in the U.S.A. and Europe today, the widely accepted opinion of governments and their populations usually depends on sets of habituated, presumably axiomatic assumptions, to such effect that nearly all of the people living within that culture behave in a way which should remind us of pet goldfish swimming within an accustomed bowl. The victims of such traditions are therefore usually unprepared to cope with a world existing beyond the bounds of those adopted assumptions. They remain content to live with those assumptions, until the time the fishbowl, so to speak, is smashed by events unforeseen in the custom of its inhabitants.

So, with rare exceptions, the most significant, but usually poorly sensed forces of history, proceed in long waves, even very long waves. The improved art of statecraft which our world needs for the present, and for the times before us, must return, away from the ruinous accumulation of present-day habits, to that kind of longer view which informed the crafters of our republic and its original Declaration of Independence and Constitution. This we must do both for the nations which are the professed heirs of European civilization, and for the others, as for ourselves alone.

That much said, now let us rejoin the performance of the second part of Aeschylus's Prometheus Trilogy, **Prometheus Bound**.

The gist of the tragic obstacle to be overcome by the dupes of the Olympian Zeus, is the following.

As long as the people who have accepted a certain culture are able to ignore the difference between the real world and the imaginary world, such as that of Zeus's realm, which their culture causes them to imagine to exist, they are satisfied to behave in a way which corresponds to the mistaken beliefs which that culture impels them to adopt. Meanwhile, the point is approaching now (if, indeed, it has not already virtually arrived), at which the discrepancy between reality and what their adopted cultures have impelled them to believe, will seem, suddenly, to explode in their faces.[2]

EIRNS/Stuart Lewis

Newt "Robespierre" Gingrich and fellow Conservative Revolutionaries on Capitol Hill, Jan. 11, 1995.

At that moment of crisis, they are astonished, at first, that what they have believed that "experience" taught them in the short run no longer works under present conditions. They are mistaken in even that opinion; actually, it never really worked in the sense they had assumed that it did; but, they are now experiencing the pain of paying for the mistake of maintaining their presently habituated opinions far too long. It was those former opinions which did not work. It was those widely accepted versions of adaptation to so-called "conventional," or "popular" opinions, which had been wrong all that time.

Sometimes the habituated illusions of a culture come and go within a lifetime. Sometimes, they persist over several generations, or longer. Most of what historians and economists have regarded as important cycles, have their origin, in large degree, in the fallacies embedded in the practiced beliefs of those who have shared that margin of popular error. The result is that, ultimately, the margin of deviation of a society's culture from reality, reaches a point that that discrepancy between belief and consequence can no longer be overlooked.

For that reason, often, as now, a wave of development which has been unfolding, but underrated, even usually unsuspected, unfolding over the greater part of a millennium, or even much longer, becomes suddenly, as during the period beginning the neo-Jacobin "Gingrich Revolution" of the 1994 U.S. Congressional election, the insistent, virtually decisive, global political

---

2. The French Revolution of 1789, and the Russian Revolution of 1917, are prime examples of this. From 1763-1776 on, the conditions leading toward the French Revolution, even some of the crucial details of the preparations, from 1783 onward, under Britain's Lord Shelburne, for orchestrating the French Revolution of July 14, 1789 and beyond, were clear to any alert observer of the roles of the circles of Philippe Egalité, Jacques Necker, and the Martinist freemasonic order. Similarly, V.I. Lenin was relatively unique in recognizing the clear evidence pointing to his voluntarist's keen foresight into the way in which the launching of a general war in Europe must lead to the fall of the Czar, the failure of the Russian would-be successors of the Czar, and the opportunity for what became the October Revolution. Similarly, the 1922-1945 reign of fascism in Europe, and the general war would have been foreseen by any literate adult person whose mind had not been blocked by a delusory attachment to the generally accepted assumptions of a then-popularized fishbowl mentality.

issue of the present moment.[3] It were as if the fishbowl had been smashed by external forces. Belief in the habits of thought associated with the hegemony of the 1763-2004 Anglo-Dutch Liberal system, is an example of the kind of delusion which leads an entire culture into the risk of the kind of systemic breakdown of that culture which could now go so far as to plunge much of this planet into what is described as a new dark age.

That is a fair mental image of the type of pathological state of mind of the typical European, or others, which has led our civilization into the present systemic crisis. A foolish system, most notably that of the recent four decades of Congress for Cultural Freedom-led degeneration of European culture, is now being overtaken by events tantamount to the smashing of the relevant, habituated popular cultural fishbowls. Those pathological states of mind are to be seen from the Classical standpoint of Aeschylus's Prometheus, as the adoption of "what they say," as a disguise for: "I am thinking in the way which Zeus demands that I think, if I do not wish to get the same treatment which Prometheus has received."

Consider the following, very brief summary of those general principles of history which underlie, and make comprehensible the kind of shocking, tectonic-like transition which, like the 1994-1995 neo-conservative—e.g., fascist—revolution of Newt "Robespierre" Gingrich, had, seemingly suddenly, overtaken the long-term trends of politics in the world in general, especially the people of the U.S.A. and Europe, during the most recent ten years. We must begin our summary of that and related contemporary cases, with a glimpse into the leading features of more than 2,500 years of European history since Thales, Pythagoras, and Solon of Athens. Only in that approach, can we make clear the patterns of historical "cycles" which have governed the evolution of European civilization up to the present time.

So, as historian Friedrich Schiller taught, and as I shall emphasize the relevant evidence here, no one could really understand the presently onrushing crisis of world civilization today, without an integrated conception of the principal processes which have governed both the good and bad features of the unfolding development of European culture since the time of Thales, Solon, Pythagoras, and Plato.

It is not until we study history for the purpose of discovering those principles which shape the way in which relatively short periods, of merely a few hundred years or so, are organized as subsumed phases of longer, millennia-long processes, that the mind is focussed in a way it is prepared to cope, intellectually, with the kinds of sudden, radical changes in circumstance and cultural trends which are sweeping down on the sundry parts of the world, and the world as a whole, just now.

Notably, for example, the influence of the Congress for Cultural Freedom, as typified by existentialist circles of depraved creatures such as Herbert Marcuse, Theodor Adorno, and Hannah Arendt, by banning a principle of truth from culture, repeated the same fatal error of Sophism which lured Athens into its ruin through the Peloponnesian War. The substitution of "democracy" for truth, which was the essence of Sophism, then and now, deprives the person who shares that ideological disorder, of the capacity to comprehend the long-wave processes of history which we must recognize if we are to control the effect of our short-term decisions on the destiny of our culture. Precisely this error of the Sophists and their intellectual cousins, led the Athens of Pericles into its self-inflicted ruin. It is this same error, as typified by the pernicious, quasi-Dionysian, *pro-counterculture* dogma of the post-war Congress for Cultural Freedom, which is largely responsible for the success with which the self-inflicted ruin of Europe and the Americas has been foisted upon those victims today.

In statecraft, as in physical science, the primary challenge and responsibility, is the thinker's ability, and willingness, to adopt an emotionally driven sense of moral responsibility for the long-term effects on future society, of the choices we make in the short term of the here and now. *Competent statecraft requires that we not make the potentially fatal mistake of even many figures who are otherwise gifted and well-meaning; we must not permit strategy (i.e., policy) to be driven by tactics, as does an otherwise able commander in battles who wins the day, but loses the war.*[4]

Then, once we have accepted that requirement, we must, as I shall also show here, now match that view of

---

3. The Gingrich "inaugural," "Contract on America" tirade of January 20, 1995.

4. An example is the case of the qualified professional U.S. military commanders sent to fight an anti-Constitutional, unjustified war in Iraq, a so-called "war without an exit strategy," in which the U.S. forces are dying now, ultimately to lose. So, in Indo-China, U.S. forces won the battles, but ultimately, inevitably, lost the war. The highest expression of strategy in military affairs, is, as General Douglas MacArthur did often in the Pacific, to win the war without fighting unnecessary battles, thus even causing the potential adversary to praise the ultimate outcome.

an integrated, millennial process of European civilization against the challenge of building a secure future for our planet, through new forms of relationship with what are broadly classed as Asian culture. Now, after thousands of years, precisely that challenge now faces us all, as never, in comparable degree, in history before this time. I continue with that point of reference in view of the horizon of the kind of development which is the pivotal point of this report.

What Is Liberal Imperialism?

Had Roosevelt lived, the U.S.A.'s power would have moved the post-war world toward freeing the planet from the vestiges of the Anglo-Dutch Liberals' colonial-imperialist system. The establishment of a planetary treaty system, under Franklin Roosevelt's Bretton Woods system, among economically progressive sovereign nation-states, would have launched a wave of development among peoples who had been formerly subject to the overreach of colonialist powers.

With the death of President Roosevelt, his successor, President Harry "Harriman" Truman, joined those same Anglo-Dutch-led Liberal-imperialist powers against which our great battle for freedom, against fascism, had been fought; Truman and his accomplices of the post-Roosevelt interval, went over, for a time, to the other side, as participants in a bloody suppression of that freedom of those "colonialized" peoples whom Roosevelt had intended to free with aid of American technology.

Now, the form of the *Liberal imperialist system*[5] of

a half-century ago and earlier, has been superseded by a more radically vicious version, the presently operating scheme, under predatory financier-oligarchical institutions such as the post-1971 International Monetary Fund and World Bank, for the eradication of the sovereignties of all of the nations of this planet: globalization. The latter is a scheme, rooted in a modern, empiricist/existentialist guise, of the same method of Sophistry which brought down Greek civilization in the Peloponnesian War, a scheme designed for modern times by the influential British strategic utopian, H.G. Wells, in his 1928 *The Open Conspiracy*. That latter scheme is the special, utopian variant of that Liberal imperial system, which has emerged in the guise of "globalization" during the recent four decades, especially since the great monetary-system changes of 1971-1981.

This Liberal imperialist form of utopian scheme is what is presently crashing, of its own weight, around the world's ears. This presently onrushing disintegration of the world's present Liberal system, the present monetary-financial system, has thrust the world into the challenge of issues which had been more easily solved sixty years ago, had Roosevelt's post-war intentions been carried out. This has presented us with the great European-Asian cultural crisis of today. That is a crisis of today, which is the outgrowth of a crucial long-term feature of the challenge erupting from the doom we have brought upon ourselves by turning away from President Franklin Roosevelt's intentions, nearly sixty years ago.

There are deep and ancient principles involved in this long wave of developments leading to the present moment, developments which, with their sometimes profound implications, must be considered as follows:

Consider the following, relevant lesson from ancient Classical Greece.

In his *Timaeus* dialogue, Plato writes of the Egyptians' accounts of the earlier existence of humanity on this planet, a view of a series of long waves of history, each punctuated by the outcome of a series of monstrously destructive dark ages. In support of that view, we can fairly estimate the possible existence of a human species as a species which is, functionally, absolutely

---

5. The proper noun, "Liberal," refers to the mode of systemic exclusion of a notion of truth, a modern form of Sophistry, which was crafted by the followers of Venice's Paolo Sarpi, the founder of modern empiricism. (Hence, exclusion of a principle of truth, is characteristic of Liberalism.) Sarpi's relevant followers include his own house lackey Galileo Galilei, England's Francis Bacon and Thomas Hobbes, and such founders of Eighteenth-Century Anglo-Dutch and French Liberalism as John Locke, Bernard Mandeville, François Quesnay, David Hume, Voltaire, d'Alembert, and Lord Shelburne's lackeys Adam Smith, Edward Gibbon, and Jeremy Bentham. The term Liberalism is interchangeable with terms such as "The Eighteenth-Century French and English Enlightenment," The Eighteenth-Century "Venetian Party," as that term were still the true name of the adopted policy of practice of the Fabian faction of the United Kingdom's Tony Blair government, "Liberal Imperialism," and of that system of indifference to a principle of truth, Kantianism. Each and all of these predecessors of the Blair government signify, precisely, the Anglo-Dutch Liberal Imperialism established on behalf of the British East India Company at the February 1763 Treaty of Paris. The American System of political-economy, as defined by U.S. Treasury Secretary Alexander Hamilton, et al., has been the truthful counter to philosophical Liberalism since the roots of the American Revolution in that February 1763 Treaty of Paris which established the

British East India Company as our nation's principal adversary, an empire of the form of Liberal Imperialism. The term "imperialist," as illustrated by British Liberal Imperialism today, signifies an attempted revival of the medieval "ultramontane" system, under which the Venetian financier oligarchy, allied with the Norman chivalry, ran the anti-nation-state system which collapsed upon itself in the Fourteenth-Century New Dark Age.

Venice's Paolo Sarpi launched the cult of empiricism, the modern form of Sophistry.

distinct from and superior to the great apes, the human species, which has existed on this planet for perhaps as long as two millions years. For example, we know with certainty, of some great natural crises in the conditions for human habitation on this planet. Among these are the series of shock effects associated with the process of melting of the preceding great glaciation over much of the Planet's Northern Hemisphere, as the levels of the oceans rose, over an interval which began about 20,000 years ago today, by a net amount of between 300-400 feet, to the present, temporarily relatively fixed levels of recent millennia which have been known to us, during the recent six millennia, as our European custom has named fairly as recorded history.[6]

As Plato emphasized there, the long waves of the existence of mankind, present us with great calamities of nature we had been unable to master at that time, but, also, terrible, man-created dark ages, such as the ominous crisis coming down on world society at this moment, a crisis which society has inflicted willfully upon itself. Neither natural nor man-made dark ages, like those of the past, will determine our future irreversibly. Superior powers available for mankind's use, exist, powers which are expressed in long waves of development of mankind. These are the types of powers which science enables us to know as having transcended great calamities of the past. These powers work to the effect of demonstrating that there is an underlying principle of development, through which something immortal from ancient peoples lives on in the world of today.

We know, thus, of something of much greater, and immediate practical importance for society today, than these powers as such. The close study of the way in which language has developed certain functional qualities specific to the functions of Classical physical science and methods of Classical artistic composition, points, as India's Tilak did, and scholars at Pune after him, too, toward well-developed features of what might be classed as the pre-historic roles of the principles of physical science and Classical non-plastic artistic composition of language-cultures.[7] It is in the transmission of knowledge of powers, by means of language-cultures developed to that effect, that the discoveries of today may acquire an immortal influence on the condition of future society. Such modern studies of the role of such factors as Classical irony in the characteristics of the use of a language, imply a means of human cultural development, by successive cultures, over spans of not only tens of thousands, but even hundreds of thousands of years.[8]

Thus, as mankind develops culturally, our species develops the ability to master more and more of even those threatened natural catastrophes which could not have been overcome willfully in earlier centuries or millennia. Cycles do not recur simply; cycles continue to appear, but, as man's cumulative power over nature increases, the possibility of willfully controlling the fate of society in face of threats from so-called natural catastrophes, is improved.[9]

Such progress calls our attention to certain evidence

---

6. With an intervening great flooding-phase of the melt, as Plato reports, about 10,000 B.C. Note recent studies of sites of habitation in the Black Sea dated from the flooding which transformed that sea from a fresh-water lake to a salt sea. These conform to the estimate given by Plato.

7. Bal Gangadhar Tilak, *Orion* (1893) and *The Arctic Home in the Vedas* (1903).

8. This is no exaggeration, no wild guess. Scientist Vladimir Vernadsky's treatment of the Noösphere points to the principled issue involved. Cf. Lyndon H. LaRouche, Jr., *The Economics of the Noösphere* (Washington, D.C.: EIR News Service, 2001). See the discussion of this below.

9. Note that this complements, in Leibniz's categorically infinitesimal calculus, the catenary-cued principle of universal physical least action.

relevant to that point. It shows us, for example, a certain uniqueness of the development of what historian Friedrich Schiller recognized as a distinct species of European culture traced through the ancient mortal conflict between the conflicting conceptions of man's nature, which separates the outlook of Solon of Athens from the wicked code of Lycurgus's Sparta. Schiller's point in his celebrated Jena lectures, is not only validated, but is of pivotal importance for the subject of this present report.[10]

In this reflection, one awesome point is outstanding. History obliges us to trace the decline of Greek culture from its acme, doing this from the standpoint represented by Plato and his Pythagorean and related predecessors, a decline which persisted with some outstanding particular exceptions, such as the work of Aristarchus, Eratosthenes, and Archimedes, until the rebirth of Classical Greek culture's treasures, during Europe's Fifteenth-Century, Italy-pivotted Renaissance.

Thus, the history of European civilization itself warns those who have come to know the principles of the modern scientific method of Nicholas of Cusa and Johannes Kepler, that the study of the principled characteristics of relatively distinct civilizations, can not be adduced by limiting attention to the evidence of a mere century, nor even hundreds of years; the characteristics of European civilization, as if in cycles, are expressed in thousands, or, as Tilak argued, traceable back even tens of thousands, of years.

The pivotal point of all of the essential argument presented in these pages, is that all human culture has a common basis in the essential distinction of the member of the human species from all other known forms of mortal life. Within these bounds, as I shall show here, the term "European civilization" has a scientifically precise, specific meaning.

It is a fortunate convenience for us, in discussing the relevant matters of this report today, that the development of the concept of the Noösphere, by Russian biogeochemist Vladimir Vernadsky, is a crucial instance of a direct return of the work of a leading modern scientist to the explicit standpoint of the pre-Aristotelean method in Classical Greek science, the standpoint of *Sphaerics*,

of the time of Thales, Solon, Pythagoras, Plato, et al.

This point is of crucial importance for discussing the central issue of this report as a whole. The connection of Vernadsky to both the modern Bernhard Riemann and the ancient Plato, is bridged by the circles associated with the role of the founder of modern European experimental science, Cardinal Nicholas of Cusa. As we shall see, more clearly, in a later portion of this report, this connection provides a strategy for approaching the need for the kinds of treaty arrangements among respectively sovereign European and Asian cultures which will do for global politics today, what the 1648 Treaty of Westphalia did for ending approximately a century and a half, from 1492 through 1648, of religious warfare in Europe.[11]

Promethean Man

The crucial challenge of an attempted European-Asian pact, even as might be presented to those relatively very few of us who are closest to the desired understanding, even among those of us inside European civilization, is not only that Asian cultures generally lack any philosophical grounding in the actually scientific, historically specific principles upon which the concept of the modern sovereign nation-state depends absolutely. The principle of the sovereign nation-state republic can not be reborn from a Xerox machine, or built under the guidance of stolen secret diagrams; it must be grown up from a living seed, as any other living organism.

The knowledge of that principle must be developed within each existing national culture, that from the universal principle common to all human nature. That principle appears as like a seed of the discovery of universal knowledge which exists within each member of a national language-culture. The development of this seed, within the process of that culture, is the only true basis for the principle of national sovereignty, the only true basis for the modern sovereign form of nation-state republic.

As can be demonstrated by observing the leading press of European nations, the conscious understanding of the relevant implications of the modern European state found among even leading intellectual circles

---

10. Schiller's inaugural lecture at Jena University, "What Is, and to What End Do We Study, Universal History?" delivered on May 26-27, 1789, is reprinted in **Friedrich Schiller: Poet of Freedom**, Vol. II (Washington, D.C.: Schiller Institute, 1988).

11. Cf. Cardinal Nicholas of Cusa, **De Pace Fidei**, in **Toward a New Council of Florence: 'On the Peace of Faith' and Other Works by Nicolaus of Cusa**, William F. Wertz, Jr., trans. (Washington, D.C.: Schiller Institute, 1993).

inside European culture today, falls way below the standard which must be met to reach an effective understanding, even a level of understanding below the standard of political-philosophical literacy expressed by the disputes of the Eighteenth and Nineteenth Centuries. The inherent sophistry of empiricism, or, worse, positivism and existentialism, is largely responsible for the present-day cultural decay within globally extended European culture generally. The recent four decades' degeneration of the level of quality of intellectual life in Europe and the Americas, on this account, must be fairly described as a monstrous exercise in galloping cultural illiteracy.

However, despite all that, literate and semi-literate cultures inside European civilization are accustomed to the effects of the notion of the sovereign nation-state republic, even if they do not understand that notion's premises in natural law; whereas, those of Asian cultures tend to brush aside those special issues which are most crucial for achieving a functionally effective understanding.

Therefore, to reach the kind of treaty agreement among nations which is needed by the world at large, and that under conditions of today's crisis, we must provide the representatives of Asian cultures with a view, made understandable to them, in their terms, of the innermost principles of the crucial, best features of the historical experience of the struggle, since Solon of Athens, to establish that form of modern European sovereign nation-state republic first achieved, in fair approximation, under France's Louis XI and England's Henry VII. [See **Figure 2**.]

That said, the most efficient approach to that task is to present the Asian intellectual leader with a shockingly clear statement on the interrelated subjects of monotheism and Promethean man. In all branches of valid modes of scientific inquiry, including statecraft, it is only through a relentless presentation of a true paradox, as in a Platonic dialogue, that the individual human mind can be prompted to generate a true conception of principle, either physical-scientific principle, or a principle of the type associated with both Classical forms of artistic composition and principles of statecraft as a derivative of the notion of such Classical forms of principles of artistic composition. What is needed at this point in history, is a European-Eurasian treaty agreement based on principle. It is the relevant meaning of principle itself, principle in the scientific sense, which must be taken into account, for this purpose.

The root-concept on which that monotheistic humanist tradition characteristic of the emergence of modern European civilization from medievalism is based, had been given such names as "the Prometheus Principle" since ancient Greece. This name references, most commonly, the circulation of the great Prometheus Trilogy of the Athens Classical tragedian Aeschylus. As I have emphasized here earlier, this Trilogy is best known to modern civilization by reference to the surviving model part of that trilogy, **Prometheus Bound**. It is in that **Prometheus Bound** that the most crucial issue of all European civilization confronts us in what is, implicitly, the most shocking and meaningful way. It must also shock the conscience of the leading representatives of Asian culture, if the desired foundations for a treaty-agreement are to be recognized on both sides.

Agreements apparently reached by means of compromising differences of principle, may appear to be the least abrasive form of negotiation, but, in the end, it is always the way in which to produce an agreement which is the most worthless in the long run: because, that approach, like attempting to compose an ecumenical drafting of a Christian Cannibal's Cookbook, evades what continue to be the ominous conflicts in principle, rather than actually resolving them.

For example, the charge was made by the fascist-like Sophists (that irrationalist Democratic Party of Athens which perpetrated the judicial murder of Socrates), that Socrates denied the gods. This charge is a typical expression of the issue posed by the Prometheus Principle of Aeschylus's Trilogy. The Roman Empire's bloody mass-murder against the Christians, from the Emperor Nero through the early part of the reign of Diocletian, is, similarly, a typical expression of what is often named as the "pagan," or the pro-pantheonic, oligarchical principle, which is characteristic of those we must come to abhor as the chief pollutant in European culture, the virtually existentialist, philosophically reductionist tradition of Greece's sophist and kindred factions.[12]

---

12. Since this report is focussed upon the subject of a system of fraternal relations among, most notably, European and Asian cultures, the working definition of "Christian" here must be precise, and rigorously defined. Therefore, when I employ the term "Christian" throughout this present and other published writings, I mean a body of belief and practice formed around such bare essentials as an informed, humanistic reading of the first chapter of Genesis, and the content of the New Testament, especially the Gospel of John and the Epistles of Paul, all as read from the vantage-point in method represented by John and Paul, the method associated with a vantage-point typified by the method of Pla-

FIGURE 2

Growth of European Population, Population-Density, and Life-Expectancy at Birth, Estimated for 100,000 B.C.–A.D. 1975

Alone among all other species, man's numerical increase is a function of increasing mastery over nature —increase of potential population-density—as reflected historically in the increase of actual population-density. In transforming his conditions of existence, man transforms himself. The transformation of the species itself is reflected in the increase of estimated life-expectancy over mankind's historical span. Such changes are primarily located in, and have accelerated over, the last six-hundred years of man's multi-thousand-year existence. Institutionalization of the conception of man as the living image of God the Creator during the Golden Renaissance, through the Renaissance creation of the sovereign nation-state, is the conceptual origin of the latter expansion of the potential which uniquely makes man what he is.

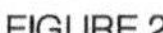

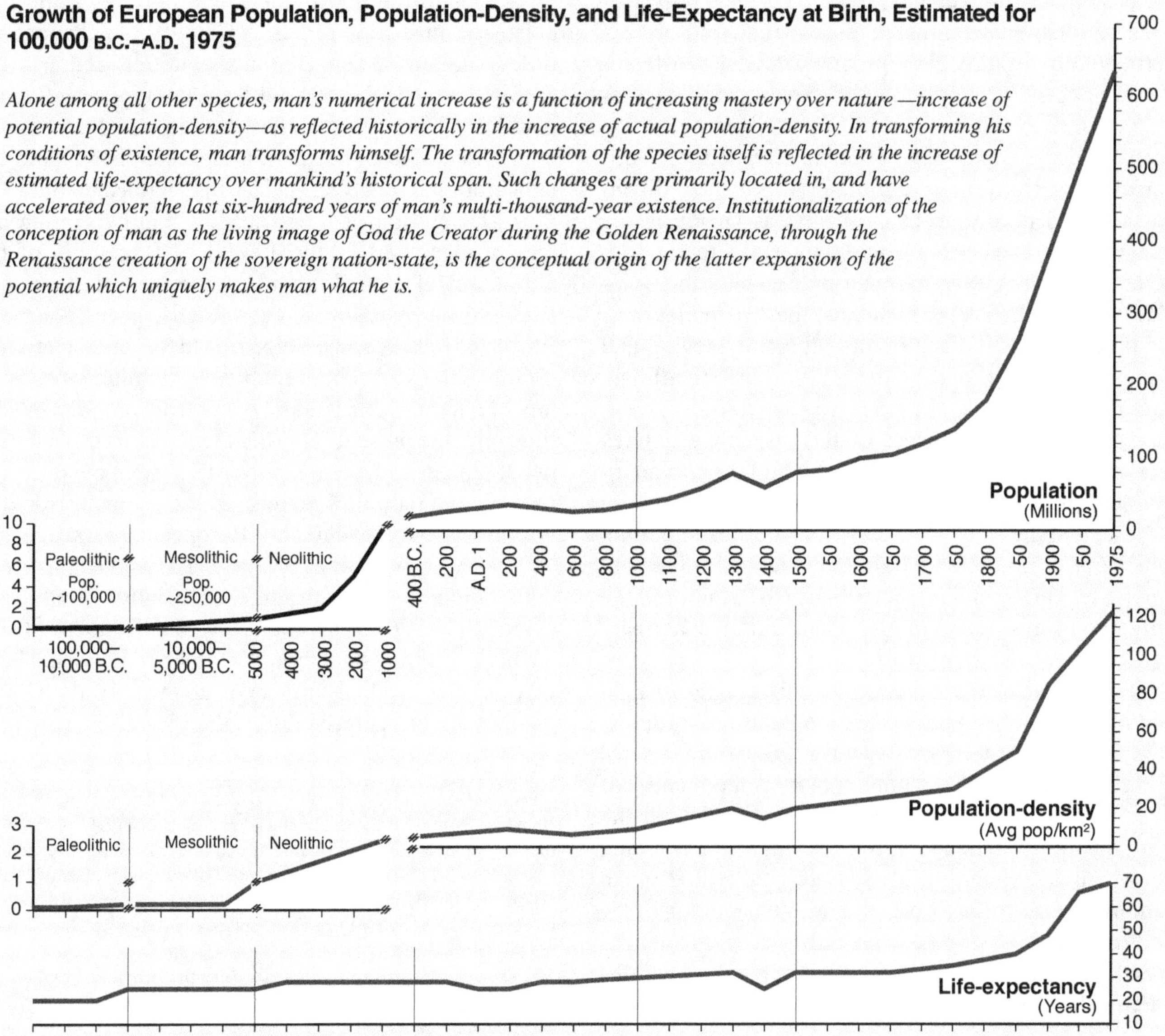

All charts are based on standard estimates compiled by existing schools of demography. None claim any more precision than the indicative; however, the scaling flattens out what might otherwise be locally, or even temporally, significant variation, reducing all thereby to the set of changes which is significant, independant of the quality of estimates and scaling of the graphs. Sources: For population and population-density, Colin McEvedy and Richard Jones, *Atlas of World Population History*; for life-expectancy, various studies in historical demography.

Note breaks and changes in scales.

That much said on this immediate point, that as a matter of indispensable preliminaries, so far, let us now proceed.

The Classical humanist argument (e.g., the Christian humanist argument) is that the individual member of the human species, is absolutely distinguished from the beasts by virtue of the innate power to discover and transmit efficient knowledge of universal physical principles, such as Johannes Kepler's unique discovery of

to's ***Timaeus*** and other dialogues. By "Christian," I mean the body of persons who either explicitly share those beliefs as defined by the Classical method employed by John and Paul, or who have accepted the effect of those beliefs in the shaping of their own beliefs and practice. Those who lack a competent knowledge of the principles of epistemology, would often describe my argument here as methodologically "idealistic," thus reflecting the tell-tale influence of radically reductionist method upon their opinions. The physical domain of Platonic method is identical with the notion of a mathematical-physical complex domain as defined in modern scientific usages by exemplars such as Carl Gauss and Bernhard Riemann.

the principle of universal gravitation.[13] The power of the individual human mind to discover and transmit experimentally validatable, efficient knowledge of universal physical principles, is the experimental expression of this crucial distinction of man from beast. On account of this capacity for efficient knowledge of universal physical principles, man is properly distinguished, essentially, from the beasts as "made in the image of the Creator," a single universal Creator who is, as Philo of Alexandria, among notable others, including Christians, argued against the Aristoteleans of his time, a God who is a living, efficiently active, and immortal presence, and a universal power for endlessly continuing change, in the universe, then as now.

This reciprocal concept of the respective natures and relationship between the Creator and the human individual, is both the essence of the best of European culture, and the only premise within European culture which makes possible a durable, ecumenical agreement among European and Asian cultures (for example), the only premise which affords Asian cultures a treaty which they could rightly trust.

The denial of the existence of this quality of man and his Creator, is expressed as the Pantheonic, or oligarchical principle. This was the same oligarchical principle which the contemporary opponents of Socrates and Plato, for example, associated with the Babylonian, or Persian Model, the oligarchical model on which the founding of the later imperial Roman Empire was notoriously based. The evil pantheon of the gods of Zeus's Olympus, Zeus as the veritable Satan of Aeschylus's Prometheus Trilogy, is typical of the oligarchical model.[14]

Although the first modern nation-states came into existence during the Fifteenth Century, the characteristic distinction of that Classical tradition of European civilization, which is traced from the typical influence of the Pythagoreans, Thales, Solon, and Plato, is the commitment, from the start, to the establishment of the constitutional republic, such as that defined by the 1776 U.S. Declaration of Independence and overriding authority expressed as the 1787-1789 Preamble of the U.S. Federal Constitution.[15] Although this goal had been but rarely realized, even briefly, in the course of European history since Solon of Athens, the intention to establish the sovereign republic as the highest body of law of a nation, existed and persisted from that ancient time until the present. This historical perspective for the development and maintenance of a system of sovereign nation-state republics, expresses the characteristic distinction, and achievement of European civilization.

The entirety of what is fairly described as European civilization, is a long struggle, especially within European cultures, to bring about the establishment of that sovereign nation-state republic which replaces the heritage of such wicked influences as those of the Olympian Zeus, the replacement of the idea of the rule over

---

"new Persian Empire" which the Christians identified as "The Whore of Babylon." None of these can be considered as "accidental," or as depicting some spontaneous decay within the culture of Athens. The culture of a people, as the most advanced current of Greek culture, that of Thales, Solon, and the Pythagoreans, was systemically corrupted by that culture's enemies, as by the Eleatics, Sophists, et al., after which the Greeks did the rest to themselves.

15. The defining principle of law on which the Benjamin Franklin-led, 1776 founding of the U.S. republic was premised, was the rejection of the principle of Anglo-Dutch Liberalism which is central to John Locke's *Essays on Human Understanding*. The mobilization of the preparations for U.S. independence, which was prompted as a reaction against the 1763 Treaty of Paris founding the British East India Company's British Empire, was centered around the international figure of Benjamin Franklin, and featured the leading influence of Leibniz's denunciation of Locke in his own *New Essays on Human Understanding*. Thus, the relevant passage from Leibniz was featured as the central affirmative principle of universal natural law stated in the Declaration of Independence: the right to "the pursuit of happiness," rather than the Lockean principle of "property" (e.g., "shareholder value") upon which the practice of slavery was premised. This was restated as the fundamental constitutional law of the Federal republic as the Preamble of the 1787-1789 Constitution. This principle of natural law (the same "common good" for which Louis XI's France and Henry VII's England were established) is the fundamental point of difference between the Constitutional law of the U.S.A. and that of western and central European states today. Under the U.S. Constitution, the existence of an independent central banking system, the hallmark of the Venetian system, is, in principle, outlawed.

---

13. Not to be confused with the "push me/beat me/pull me" notions of Cartesian and related dogmas.

14. The awful aftermath of the Peloponnesian War, prompted the search for a new empire modelled upon that of the Mesopotamian empires, an empire combining the reaches of Greek, Egyptian, and Middle Eastern cultures. This attempt was "judoed" by the followers of Plato in the Academy of Athens, who associated themselves with the cause of Philip of Macedon's son and Aristotle's adversary, Alexander, resulting in the dissolution of the Achaemenid empire, and the temporary domination of the eastern Mediterranean by a Hellenistic culture, which was dominated culturally, in turn, by a Classical Greek legacy of the Platonic Academy of Athens and Cyrenaica (e.g., that of Eratosthenes) now centered in Ptolemaic Egypt. The establishment of the "new Persian Empire," thus came about through an agreement between Octavian (later Augustus Caesar) and the priests of the Mithra cult, struck on the Isle of Capri, subsequently the sacred possession of the Caesars, until approximately A.D. 500. The cult of Mithra's support of Octavian, against Antony and Cleopatra, settled the issue of who would run that

man and his universe by a reigning immortal oligarchy, by a system of a form of sovereign nation-states based on the notion of the human individual as set absolutely apart from, and above the beasts. This is a human individual made as a creative intellect in the likeness of, and servant of a single living Creator, and held responsible, by that Creator, for the ordering of, and rule over the improvement of the universe which mankind inhabits. In other words, the crucial issue of all European culture is expressed by the resistance of the human hero, Prometheus, against the evil oligarchy typified by the Olympian Zeus.

Thus, this principle of the sovereign republic bears the burden of one qualification, the burden of natural law as implicitly defined by Plato's set of dialogues. This brings our attention back to the specific matters posed by use of the term "Promethean man."

The conflict between the Olympian Zeus of Aeschylus's Trilogy and Prometheus, is the charge that Prometheus supplied the people with the knowledge of the use of fire.

Empiricism: Zeus as Satan

The issue is that oligarchy's passion, whether as the image of Zeus's fantastic Olympus, or modern European reductionist philosophies such as empiricism or the ranting of the followers of Bertrand Russell and the existentialists, who deny that man has the power to discover and employ those universal physical principles, which are experimentally demonstrable to be universal physical principles, but which can not be known directly by means of bare sense-perception. That issue is otherwise expressed in statecraft, by the repressive struggle, by the living oligarchy, to halt the commitment of modern civilization to those forms of scientific progress which increase man's power, per capita, over the universe we inhabit: to impose an oppressive system, contrary to man's nature, in which scientific-technological progress by mankind is banned as evil, as the pagan Olympian Zeus of the Aeschylus Trilogy condemned Prometheus, on that precise issue.

In forbidding man the knowledge of universal physical principles, such as the principle of fire and its use, Zeus condemned mankind to live as a beast, not a creature made in the image of the Creator. That is, precisely, the Satanic principle. Modern empiricism does the same thing in a slightly different way, but with the same ultimate result, as we have seen in the recent four decades of collapse of European civilization under the

anti-science, "back to nature" cults, a kind of "social disease"—"the syphilis of the counterculture"—which took over more and more of the young-adult populations, beginning the second half of the 1960s.

The intent of the cult of empiricism launched by Venice's Paolo Sarpi, to this effect, was shown, fully naked, by the cult-circles of Bertrand Russell and such followers as his devoted acolytes Norbert Wiener and John von Neumann. By arguing that all scientific knowledge could be derived from a brutishly arithmetic notion of algebraic functions, Russell sought, with plainly expressed intent, to halt the progress of science, by banning the method by means of which discoveries of experimentally valid universal physical principles could be replicated by students and others.[16]

This was not, however, original to Russell; it was the standard dogma of the Seventeenth and Eighteenth Centuries' Anglo-Dutch Liberal cult, and the foundation for the Physiocratic hoax which Adam Smith plagiarized from the work of France's François Quesnay and Turgot. The particular significance of Quesnay on this account, is that he insists frankly on the argument that the farmers of the feudal landlord's estate are of the same rank as herded cattle. This assumption is the essential part of Adam Smith's doctrine of "free trade," but was also the essential argument in Smith's 1759 publication, *The Theory of the Moral Sentiments*, as also the social doctrine of Galileo Galilei's student Thomas Hobbes.

This repression of the knowledgeable participation in scientific and related progress by the great mass of the poorer people, is the force for evil which confronts us as new threats of fascism inside European civilization today, and presently serves as the political motive for so-called "pro-environmentalist" changes in global civilization, which would, by their very nature, unleash, at this time, the greatest known holocaust in all human existence, the reduction of the human population from over six billions persons to a beastly rabble of less than

---

16. This was the issue which prompted the circles of Russell, including John von Neumann, to destroy scientist Kurt Gödel personally, on account of Gödel's 1931 *On Formally Undecidable Propositions of Principia Mathematica* and Related Systems, in *Kurt Gödel Collected Works*, Vol. I (New York: Solomon Fefermann, 1986), pp. 144-195. Gödel's thesis is notable among those scientific works which aimed successfully at discrediting such radical positivist hoaxes as Norbert Wiener's doctrine of Information Theory and the von Neumann-Morgenstern hoax published as *Theory of Games and Economic Behavior*. MIT's RLE is among the notable cult-centers of these offshoots of Russell's radically irrationalist dogma.

a half-billions, mostly depraved, short-lived persons, subsisting in ways suggestive of troops of baboons.

This contemporary perversion of practiced European culture expresses the doctrine of the Olympian Zeus. This is the doctrine of modern empiricism. This was the issue underlying Carl Gauss's 1799 doctoral dissertation's attack on the vicious error of the empiricists d'Alembert, Euler, Lagrange, et al., on the issue of the Fundamental Theorem of Algebra, and also of Gauss's suppression, out of fear of persecution, of his own contributions to the discovery of an anti-Euclidean geometry (rather than a non-Euclidean one such as that of Lobachevsky and Janos Bolyai).

Man is distinguished from, and above the beasts by reason. By reason, we signify the power to discover universal physical principles, as no beast can replicate this. This is a correlative of the argument to the same effect by Vernadsky's defining the experimental proof of principle of the existence of the Noösphere: that the human mind is capable of knowing and acting upon the power to make categorical changes in the ordering of the universe, beyond what is possible with the bounds, respectively, of the abiotic domain and the Biosphere.

Thus man is, at once, a mortal being, as animals are; but, man also performs a function in the universe which is higher than that of any form of mortal life, the creative power associated experimentally with the effects of the Noösphere. This creative power, generated by the human identity of a single person, is transmitted as a power, as an effect to others and to future generations. It is the efficient transfer of knowledge of this universal quality, across time, to future generations, which, rather than the mortal flesh, is the primary subject of the human personal identity. This is the immortal soul of Plato's *Phaedo* and Moses Mendelssohn's *Phaedon*. This human identity is the proper subject of social relations, the only competent basis for the notion of society, and the principle from which the requirement of a form of society known as a sovereign nation-state committed to the promotion of the general welfare of mankind, is derived.

Thus, the issue posed by Prometheus is the same as that of the intention of the *Republic* expressed by Solon of Athens and the combined work of Plato's dialogues. This has been the great achievement of the Fifteenth-Century birth of the still-imperilled, modern European nation-state republic: a form of society efficiently committed to the conscious participation of all of the people in the ordering of, and enjoyment of scientific and cultural progress of the general human condition. Without comprehension of the Prometheus issue in those terms of reference, there could not be a clear intention of principle on which to found a treaty-organization efficiently dedicated to the aims of a community of modern sovereign nation-states.

2. The Nation-States of the U.S.A. & Europe

Now it is time to make clear the functionally elementary differences between modern European and Asian cultures.

Modern European civilization began with changes typified, and also largely shaped, by the writings of the Fifteenth-Century Cardinal Nicholas of Cusa, writings which, among their other leading effects, launched the Portuguese and Spanish explorations of the Americas and of the eastbound Indian Ocean route from the South Atlantic, around the southern tip of Africa, but, more fundamentally, revived the work of such as Dante Alighieri and Petrarca in a manner and degree which established the foundations for building the long-sought efforts, since Alcuin and Charlemagne, for the actual establishment of what became the modern European sovereign nation-state.

Cusa's *Concordantia Catholica* provided the crucial starting-point for all of this, through the influence of that work on the councils, concluding on the great ecumenical Council of Florence of both the western and eastern European churches. Cusa, who played a crucial contributing role in the preparations for that Council of Florence itself, was also the founder of the modern experimental science of Luca Pacioli, Leonardo da Vinci, and Johannes Kepler, beginning his *De Docta Ignorantia*. His writings were directly responsible for launching the great transoceanic explorations of the close of that century, and were the specific inspiration for Christopher Columbus's successful transit of the Atlantic, aided by consultations with, and a map produced by, Cusa's collaborator Paolo del Pozzo Toscanelli, a map made possible by the earlier discoveries of the Platonic Academy's Eratosthenes, such as his measuring the great circle of the Earth.

These Renaissance developments took place in the aftermath of the terrible New Dark Age of the previous century. These achievements expressed the revolutionary Fifteenth-Century turn of European civilization to the launching of a true Renaissance of civilization,

A World Bank labor-intensive coal-mining project in Digwadih, India. "The great mass of poverty in those leading nations of Asia, for which no clear remedy is yet in view, must touch the conscience of the world."

away from the reductionist and obscurantist standpoint of medieval Aristoteleanism and the like, to the rebirth of the shattered institution of the Christian church from the ashes of medieval, Romantic *ultramontanism*, and the rekindling of the light of science and statecraft on the foundations of the work of Plato. These developments broke Europe free from both the dark legacies of the two Roman Empires, and from medieval Venetian-Norman *ultramontane* tyranny and its evil, Roman-esque Crusades. That Renaissance accomplished this benefit by launching the resumption of the Platonic tradition of Classical scientific practice, and a return to the Platonic, Christian principle of *agapē* (the common good). It was on the basis of this work, in which Cusa played a leading role, that the preconditions for that century's founding of the first true nation-states were subsequently established, successively, in Louis XI's France and Henry VII's England.

The crucial feature of these Fifteenth-Century changes was not only the repudiation of the traditional division of society between rulers and masses of virtual human cattle; it was the assumption of the positive responsibility for the common good by the modern state, as typified by Louis XI's France. It was the adoption of the responsibility, by the sovereign state, to develop the economy in ways expressed as the adoption of the state's responsibility for the systematic promotion of the raising of the productive powers of labor, as France's devel-

opment under Louis XI typifies this change. Henry VII's England continued that policy of emphasis upon technological and related general improvement of the productive powers of labor, thus breaking a long tradition, as from the decrees of the Roman Emperor Diocletian, of imposing virtual zero technological growth on the general economic practice of the population. This kind of break from what has been sometimes described by the morally ugly euphemism of "traditional society," is a crucial feature of the qualitative change which marks the emergence of modern European civilization from the brutish aftermath of Europe's Fourteenth-Century New Dark Age.

Although this Fifteenth-Century and ensuing developments mark the emergence of modern European civilization, it is also clear that the basis for this change is rooted in approximately two millennia of the internal struggles and development of European civilization, since no later than the lifetime and work of Thales, Solon, and Pythagoras. Despite the setbacks in European history since then, European civilization embodies a transmission and development of culture which is a continuing process of development, at least in the crucial sense of the transmission of culture over successive generations of the development of language-cultures. Thus, the emergence of modern European civilization in Europe's Fifteenth-Century Renaissance, is an expression of a developmental cultural process which is now continuing over more than 2,500 years to this present date, with roots of that development in other cultures also reaching back much, much further, as the implications of the astronomical (e.g., *Sphaerics* design of the great pyramids of Egypt attest.

Moreover, although there is class/caste form of poverty in European culture, that of a type which must be associated with the notion of a class of people held in the status of "human cattle," the failure of modern European civilization's role so far, has been that we have yet to act in ways needed to assist the world as a whole to break through that traditional cultural barrier extant within Asian cultures generally. This problem, typical of the Iberian Americas, Africa, and Asia, is a distinction which is not merely a quantitative one, but shows itself in contemporary life to be the result of an unresolved susceptibility, a result expressed as a qualitative, caste-like distinction in cultural type. The great mass of poverty in those leading nations of Asia, for which no clear remedy is yet in view, must touch the conscience of the world. The problems of China and India today, when considered in light of the actual progress which has occurred within those nations, are typical of the unresolved, dreamy challenge for which no adequate solution has been actually in reach until now. Under a continuation of the trends of the recent four decades of this planet's history, that challenge would never, never be solved, despite all wishful projections of a better future much heard from those and other parts of the world today.

To understand the cause of such afflictions in Asia, look, for example, within the U.S.A., where we have, still today, two, large-scale, well-defined caste-like distinctions existing within large rations of the population as a whole. One, among a large portion of the descendants of former African slaves. A second, among Spanish-speaking populations bearing the caste-like scars of a heritage of a Spanish system of peonage long imposed upon the indigenous population of Mexico and other places. Although we also have a heritage of Frederick Douglass and many others more or less like him, we have left a broad mass of our people, still today, bearing the scars of a self-inflicted tradition of caste-like cultural "inferiority."

It is this type of problem, as it occurs inside the U.S.A., or on other continents, which is something of which society everywhere must be cured, to establish a culture of true citizenship among the generality of the people of a national culture. Such a fault, which does occur as a blemish on contemporary European civilization, is the nature of the systemic inequity which persists, by aid of the cheap labor policies of globalization, as a widespread characteristic of Asian culture as such today. It is the development of nations to the effect of overcoming this cruel inequity suffered by relatively very large rations of the population, which is the symptomatic expression of the challenge to the human conscience of the need for Asian development today.

The conditions against which I complain exist in both Asian and European cultures. Yet, although the history of each area has its specific characteristics, the continuation of this kind of problem, in each relevant part of the world, is a reflection of the continuing evils in the present global system whose characteristics are currently expressed, actually as a trend in motion since 1964-1967, by the post-1971 IMF/World Bank system.

All of us who have had relevant experience of this in Asia (for example), share our knowledge of what we mean by our expression of concern on this account. To see the way in which relatively very large rations of the populations in various parts of the world are forced to live, from generation to generation, is something a civilized conscience can not accept as to be taken in stride. Instant solutions may not be available, but the adoption of efficiently shaped goals by those of us who think by the measure of successive generations, is nonetheless imperative. The improvements we can provide the living, are painfully modest, but what we could and must promise their posterity must be made real for foreseeable times to come. We are a species of immortal beings, on which account we can be patient where the mere beasts are not. Being immortal beings, we can draw satisfaction from our descendants' achievements, but, that does not mean that those achievements must not be real enough, not merely consoling illusions, not mere slogans: that we may justly take satisfaction from them while we are still living, today. It were immoral to promise the future pensions which present greed is presently reaching to steal—in both the U.S.A. and Europe, among other locations.

As I have pointed out earlier in this report, the period from 1492, with impassioned anti-semite and Grand Inquisitor Tomás de Torquemada's expulsion of the Jews from Spain (the precedent for the action of Adolf Hitler),[17] until the 1648 Treaty of Westphalia, the struggle to establish a system of modern sovereign nation-states in Europe, was drowned in a Venetian-orchestrated orgy of religious warfare, warfare aimed to butcher and eradicate the work of the ecumenical Council of Florence and the existence of the modern sovereign nation-state. Thus, the survival of the idea of the nation-state nominally committed to the common good specified by the 1648 Treaty of Westphalia,[18] represented a revolution in civilization as a whole, the resuscitation of the modern sovereign nation-state following

---

17. I have frequently dated the period of religious warfare to the defeat, by betrayal, of the anti-Venice League of Cambrai, which actually set religious warfare as such into motion. However, the impassioned policy for such killing-waves in pre-Treaty of Westphalia Europe, was actually set by the act of 1492, expelling the Jews from Spain in a way which we must see echoed in Hitler's expulsion and mass-murder of German Jews (in particular).

18. Cf. Cardinal Nicholas of Cusa, *De Pace Fidei*, op. cit.

its attempted suffocation, by religious wars, over a period of a century and a half.

Against that general background, of past and present on this planet, the struggle within globally extended European civilization since the great ecumenical Council of Florence, especially since Venice's strategically motivated orchestration of the Ottoman conquest of Constantinople, has been a great struggle between the forces of the modern sovereign nation-state republic and the reactionary forces of Venice and its outgrowths in the effort, led by the usurious Venetian financier oligarchy, to crush the modern sovereign nation-state in favor of some rebirth of the global reign of a new Roman (e.g., Babylonian) empire. This was the result typified by the British Empire set into motion by that watershed event known as the February 10, 1763 Treaty of Paris, established by the Eighteenth-Century, Anglo-Dutch Venetian Party. That empire's intended design is that described by the utopian doctrine of Lord Shelburne's lackey Gibbon.

The history of the world since 1763, has been essentially a great struggle between those forces which, on the one side, have been committed to the establishment and prosperity of a system of respectively sovereign nation-state republics, as best typified by the creation of the U.S. republic, and those, on the other side, such as the consummately evil Bertrand Russell, determined to crush the sovereign nation-state out of existence. All of the wars and related afflictions which this planet has suffered since 1492 have been chiefly a reflection of that great modern struggle between good and evil.

However, none of this could be competently understood, unless we adopt the long view of that development of the European civilization which began with what I have indicated as the relevant developments in ancient Greece. Thus, Solon's letter rebuking his fellow-citizens, serves as a bench-mark for the birth of the idea of the republic as realized in the 1776 U.S. Declaration of Independence and 1787-1789 Federal Constitution. Solon's "letter" is the identifiable beginning of a coherent process, called European civilization, a process defined as a struggle between, on the one side, the forces dedicated to bringing a true republic, consistent with Solon's stated intention, into being, and, on the opposing side, forces which were determined to prevent the existence of such a form of society. Hence, historian Friedrich Schiller's emphasis, in his Jena lectures, on the conflict between the doctrines of Lycurgus's Sparta and Solon's Athens.[19]

The Italy-centered, Fifteenth-Century Renaissance, which gave us the escape from a long nightmare, into modern civilization, was a product of a struggle to that end which had been the entire preceding sweep of European history. This Renaissance was a crucial turning-point in the entirety of world history. This produced a new form of society, but one which carried within it the ongoing tumult of all of the accumulated elements of the seeds of dissonance which have been experienced since the Fifteenth-Century developments, but also a form of society whose emergence has changed the history of the world in an absolute way, a change which could not be reversed without plunging all of our planet into a deep and prolonged, new dark age.

In point of fact, the recent decades' developments in Asia, typified by India and China, are not an alternative to European civilization. These nations are an integral part of the present, Anglo-Dutch-Liberal-dominated world system, and, as I shall indicate in the course of this report, could not continue to exist presently as stable nations outside the framework of a much-needed great, global reform of modern European civilization. In point of fact, all parts of the world today, are, for the moment, at least, subsidiaries of a single global monetary-financial system, to the included effect that the relative prices of both real and fictitious objects in trade are an integral, subsidiary part of that monetary-financial system.

In the case of the actualization of the presently onrushing general monetary-financial blow-out, all of the sundry elements of a complexly integrated world system, including the most notable nations of Asia, would be plunged into chaos in a way most nearly resembling the plunge of Fourteenth-Century Europe into its notorious New Dark Age.

What prevents most among what were presumably well-informed circles of finance and government, from seeing this fact, is that they are gripped, hysterically, by the fearful delusion that a crash of the type which is now onrushing simply would never happen. In fact, unless certain radical changes of the type I would propose were taken, the crash deemed unthinkable by most today will happen, very soon.

The U.S.A. versus the Empire

As I have emphasized here earlier, the combination of the religious wars of 1492-1648, the rise of the An-

---

19. Op. cit.

glo-Dutch Liberal system, and the French Revolution and its aftermath, has, so far, prevented the emergence of a durable form of true sovereign nation-state in Europe. For a time, since the July 14, 1789, the repercussions of the developments broke France's close ties to the U.S.A.,[20] and drove formerly sane and brilliant U.S. patriots such as Thomas Jefferson and Dolly's James Madison into a state of confusion. Through the revolutions of 1848, the U.S.A. itself struggled to avoid falling into a role of partisanship, one way or the other, on the issues of the quarrel between the British system and the Habsburg-dominated Europe and the world.[21] The fall of Metternich, and the mutual ruin of the nations of western and central Europe by two World Wars, ensured the relatively increased global supremacy of British monetary-financial system, except for a period of clear U.S. supremacy, from the beginning of World War II into the

Franklin D. Roosevelt Library

President Franklin D. Roosevelt. The dramatic and necessary changes required today, to a perspective in line with FDR's global objectives, will only be possible when the fact of the current imminent danger is frankly perceived by relevant leading circles.

self-inflicted decline of U.S. leadership which has been ongoing over the recent forty years. Thus, Europe today, is still dominated by the relics of a parliamentary system of government, all under the overlordship of a Venetian Party's financier-oligarchical system.

During this interval, from the beginning of the struggle for an independent U.S. republic, which developed rapidly during the decade following the establishment of the British Empire at the 1763 Treaty of Paris, there has been a continuing, ultimately mortal struggle, between the U.S. republic, on the one side, and our republic's principal mortal adversaries, the Anglo-Dutch Liberal imperialists and Britain's sometime leading European rival, and ally against the U.S. republic, the already-declining Habsburg imperial power of the early Nineteenth Century. Since the London-directed siege of the Paris Bastille, on July 14, 1789, until President Abraham Lincoln's victories of 1863-65, the U.S. was largely cut off from the support it had enjoyed during the period of our national struggle for freedom from British imperial power.

London's later deployment of its French puppet, Napoleon III, and a Habsburg, as tools of an attempted British flanking operation in Lord Palmerston's support of London's Confederate forces, during the later phase of the U.S. Civil War of 1861-65, typifies the continuing alliance of the anti-nation-state forces of Europe against the existence of the U.S.A. and its influence. This changed for the better during the period from the defeat of the Confederacy throughout the period preceding Theodore Roosevelt's accession to the U.S. Presidency. The hatred of President Franklin Roosevelt by the British government and its U.S. financier-based assets, despite the two powers' war-time alliance against Hitler, is congruent with the fact that, as U.S. General Billy Mitchell alluded to this during his famous court-martial hearing, Japan's naval attack of 1941 on Pearl Harbor, was a project which the U.S. military,

---

20. The Bastille affair was organized, and armed by Benjamin Franklin's long-standing arch-enemy and London asset, Philippe Egalité, as an election rally on behalf of British agent Jacques Necker's candidacy for Prime Minister of France. This was the first major action taken to effect a break between France and its U.S. ally of the Revolutionary War period, an action directed more immediately against the Marquis de Lafayette and the scientist Sylvain Bailly.

21. Contrary to the myth-making of even senior U.S. historians who ought to have known better, the developments of 1789-1814 in Europe had a devastating degree of disorienting effect on what had been the core of the U.S. leadership which had been crafted by Benjamin Franklin. President John Adams was disoriented by a hoax, a book called *The Roots of the Conspiracy*, by a British spy Sir John Robison, while Abigail Adams, the President's wife, became a destructive influence in her ranting against President George Washington's closest collaborator, Alexander Hamilton. Jefferson went the other way, toward the French revolutionaries. President Washington's farewell warning against foreign entanglements was not intended as a policy for all time, but referenced specifically the situation in Europe at that time, and the disorientation of formerly clear-headed patriots such as Jefferson, Adams, and Madison. It was the emergence of the Whigs, around Henry Clay, Monroe, and the increasing leadership role of John Quincy Adams, which laid the foundations for the important achievements of the U.S.A. during a period of now nearly two centuries.

prior to the Pearl Harbor attack, had filed at the time under secret U.S. war plans "Red" and "Orange," an attack which had been planned by Britain and Japan, as an option, during the period of the 1920s Naval Power negotiations. The forces representing the oligarchical tradition within Europe, are a continuing source of often feverish irrational anti-Americanism today, even sometimes from surprising circles.

With the U.S. defeat of London's Confederacy asset, British imperial policy had shifted away from further attempts at direct or covert military operations against the U.S., to a policy of Anglo-Dutch Liberal subversion. The hatred of the U.S.A. by the Fabian Liberal Imperialist faction associated with H. G. Wells and Bertrand Russell, was the more extreme expression of this British hatred against the United States. The relatively more cautious approach to subversion was through connections with Liberal channels to influential anglophile financier-oligarchical circles inside the U.S., such as those associated with the "kindergarten" of Harvard University-based Nashville Agrarian William Yandell Elliott, with the objective of assimilating a tamed and corrupted U.S.A. into a British Commonwealth. The witticism, that the U.S.A. and the U.K. are two nations divided against one another by a common language, is actually quite apt (a common language facilitates the practice of exchange of insults and trade in espionage between two rival powers).

To sum up the crucial point to be made here: From the beginning of the 1763-1789 American struggle for independence from its British imperial oppressors, modern European civilization has been chiefly divided within by two leading, opposing forces of modern European civilization: the U.S. commitment to a system of respectively sovereign nation-state republics, versus the imperial impulses and objectives of that Venetian Party represented by the Anglo-Dutch Liberal system of financier-oligarchical rule.

Of these two opposing forces, the American System of political-economy was always the superior system, morally and physically, a system conceived in the service of political freedom of the individual. This was made clear by the victory of the President Abraham Lincoln-led U.S.A. over London's Confederacy pawn. During the interval 1861-1876, the interval concluding with the U.S. Philadelphia Centennial Exposition, the U.S. emerged as the world's leading nation-state economy, rivalled only by the combined imperial resources of the British monarchy.

As a consequence of this, from 1877 onward, leading nations of Eurasia, such as Germany, Russia, and Japan, in addition to other states of the Americas, adopted crucially distinguishing, industrial and other features of the American System of Franklin, Hamilton, the Careys, and Frederick List. It was to crush the upsurge of modern economies developing in emulation of the American model, that the British monarchy of Edward VII organized what became the fratricidal "Great War" of 1914-1917: a war cast in the image of the Seven Years' War by aid of which Britain had triumphed in February 1763. Foolish Presidents Theodore Roosevelt and Ku Klux Klan fanatic Woodrow Wilson, whose passions were molded in fond recollections of the Confederacy, drew us into that war from which prudent patriotic U.S. traditions would have withheld support, a U.S. error which laid the foundations for the strategic menaces to which we have either been subjected, or have subjected ourselves, since.

Similarly, during the 1920s and early 1930s, the curiously prevalent tendency on the side of the relevant British schemers, was to keep the U.S. A. out of their plans for the coming new world war in Europe, for fear that the powerful U.S. economy might take over domination of Europe, displacing British imperial interests. This changed significantly only when London perceived Stalin's diplomatic maneuvers to encourage Russia's most immediate mortal enemy, Hitler's Germany, to choose to strike westward first, rather than eastward; on that thought, Edward VIII was ceremoniously dumped, and the British began more and more, especially after Chamberlain's performance at Munich, to see the Nazi development as strategically more immediately worrying than a period of U.S. hegemony, although some, who need not be listed here, preferred a pact with Hitler—or was it, perhaps, Hermann Göring—as late as May 1940.

The point to be emphasized here, is that, underneath expressed sentimentalities of Europeans toward Americans and vice versa, the outward similarities of the forms of economy which Asia might see in Europe and the U.S.A. are largely superficial, and the differences exist in a very significant manner and degree. Nonetheless, despite the opposite constitutional intentions of the U.S. and British systems, recent and contemporary circumstances have produced the effect of blending the immiscible into a frothy pudding, a so-called Anglo-American expression of the Anglo-Dutch Liberal system.

Now, to the degree that the Anglo-American utopian adversaries of the Franklin Roosevelt tradition, have secured temporary domination over transatlantic strategic and monetary-financial power, including inside the U.S.A. itself, the world system is dominated by the instrumentalities of a morally and economically degenerating Anglo-American financier-oligarchical cabal of Anglo-Dutch Liberalism, which has, most emphatically, presided over four decades of presently terminal decadence of its increasingly globalized world system, its virtual empire in fact.

It is of urgent importance to note here, that the only chance for the U.S. to escape a general collapse of the U.S. itself, would be to shift its national strategic perspective now, to establishing a new world monetary-financial system with global objectives akin to those which President Franklin Roosevelt had intended, as planetary perspectives, for the immediate post-war period. Such a dramatic change could occur, of course, only under the most extraordinary pressures from events, only when it were clear to the relevant leading circles that a shift to an echo of a Franklin Roosevelt perspective for the world at large is the only real alternative to a hopeless sort of general global breakdown crisis of the economy of the planet as a whole. Those imminent conditions for solving the crisis presently exist objectively, but it were necessary that that ominous fact of that imminent danger be frankly perceived subjectively.

The common feature of this present global system, as it has developed since the 1971-1972 break from the post-war fixed-exchange-rate, regulated monetary system, to a floating-exchange-rate, largely deregulated system, is the supremacy of the present, predatory form of monetary-financial system itself. However, underneath that latter umbrella of the presently largely "globalized" world system as a whole, there are important, historically determined, principled varieties of functional differences among what far too many statesmen and others mistakenly interpret as the apparently converging systems of which the world system as a whole is comprised.

The complications which arise in attempting to explain the present world system, or its parts, from the standpoint of monetary-financial evidence, are that these respectively different systems of which the world's system is composed, have influenced the evolution of one another in several manners and degrees. This mixing is partly real, but, also, in the final analysis, deceptive.

For example, all European systems of modern nation-states, including those of the Americas, do, in fact, stem from a common root in the Fifteenth-Century Renaissance establishment of a new kind of institution, the sovereign nation-state republic which is either committed to, or pretends to be committed to the common good (e.g., general welfare). Philosophically, the U.S. patriot has no essential quarrel with France's Louis XI, or England's Henry VII and Sir Thomas More, or William Shakespeare. (With Henry VIII, things begin to be complicated, and with Francis Bacon and Thomas Hobbes, much worse.)

The principal differentiation is between the British system and the American System of political-economy, derived essentially from the combined legacy of the U.S. Declaration of Independence and original Federal Constitution, a U.S. which was founded as a truly sovereign nation-state republic. This U.S. system is distinguished from European systems, which are forms of parliamentary systems of merely nominal independence, systems which have been reformed to conform to the overreaching requirements of the usurious overlordship of a global system of so-called independent central banking systems, an overlordship centered in the City of London.

However, despite transatlantic differences which are often as much axiomatic as sentimental, North America and Europe have affected one another such that each part of that combined system has been developed in ways such that each has affected the shaping of many of the internal characteristics of the other. It is urgent that it be recognized, that these systemic, apparent similarities lie essentially in the physical-economic conditions, as distinct from, and largely opposed to the constitutional underpinnings of the respective monetary-financial systems.

The essential difference between the European and U.S.A. system is constitutional, a difference in principle. The principal other differences are reflections of the fact that the U.S. economic system is premised on what is termed the American System of political-economy, which, despite its presently continuing corruption by the Federal Reserve System, presumes constitutional national sovereignty over its monetary-financial system, whereas the European systems (excluding discussion of the Soviet system here) have a Venetian financier-oligarchical heritage, expressed today as subordination of government to the power of so-called independent central banking systems, systems which are essentially masks for predatory private financier-oligarchical interests.

For example, even despite such traditional differences in political culture, post-1945 Germany adapted with such superior efficiency, relative to other European nations, to its economic reconstruction under precedents taken from the experience of the Franklin Roosevelt Administration. There are important elements of the American System of political-economy such as the still lingering role of the Kreditanstalt für Wiederaufbau today. The most notable difference between the existing European systems and the American System, is that President Franklin Roosevelt reacted to the Depression by putting the banking system through reorganization, which saved the American system of government, whereas the financier oligarchy of 1920-1945 Europe put the governments through forms of reorganization which converged upon fascism.[22]

Today, it is neither necessary, nor desirable that European states repeat the awful consequences of their earlier, pre-1945 submission to the private financier interests' central banking systems. Were they to refuse to submit now, as they should, the chances of saving both those nations, and civilization generally, would be greatly improved. If they do not refuse, then that tradition will die with the nation which refused to make the needed change in doctrine.

Thus, in summary of this point, the U.S. political establishment of (especially) the recent four decades, and the extreme right-wing utopians, have been of that disposition since the death of Franklin Roosevelt, the U.S. financial-political establishment has been definitely oriented to sharing an imperial form of world power with the British imperial establishment. Globalization is the current form of expression of that decadent intention.

____

22. Franklin Roosevelt's early- through middle-1930s adversaries, in the financier-oligarchical circles of both London and New York, had been ready to jump into bed with Mussolini, first, and then Hermann Göring's Hitler, even as late as May 1940. They had, in fact, put Mussolini and Hitler into power. Roosevelt's success depended upon his bitter political adversary, Winston Churchill, who represented those in Britain who would have preferred Hitler, but would not allow Hitler to gobble up the British Empire. Even then, had a Hitler hoping for a deal with his British aristocratic admirers, not held back the Wehrmacht tanks at Dunkirk, the war as a whole would have taken a different character. The original Anglo-French plan had been to have Hitler strike east, first, and, then, once Germany's forces were mired there, strike Germany from the west, as U.S. Walter Lippmann proposed, "expertly" after the fact. Stalin's sense of this intention, prompted the Hitler-Stalin Pact and Hitler's consequent strike west first.

3. The Differences Between Europe and Asia

Once we have taken those cited and related varieties of complications into account, the most essential points of systemic distinctions, and similarities between the American and European systems of economy, are to be recognized by lifting the monetary-financial carpeting, to see the floorboards of non-monetary, physical economy underneath. Once the monetary-financial wrappings are put aside, certain crucial similarities of principle and practice shared by the American and western and central European economies shine forth. Then, the remaining systemic differences between the Hamiltonian American System of political-economy and Liberal-dominated European systems, are chiefly reflections of the superimposition of forms of monetary-financial systems which are based upon submission to that Venetian principle expressed by so-called "independent" central banking systems. The similarities, to which I shall give attention later in this present report, reflect the physical-economic processes upon which the Venetian principle had been superimposed through the Anglo-Dutch Liberal's control over the dominant elements of the world's monetary-financial systems.

Later in this chapter of the report, I shall describe certain of those features of the European system and its most important complications from the standpoint of a science of physical economy, rather than drowning in the intellectual quicksand of attempting to explain a physical economy from an axiomatically monetary-financial standpoint.

Yet, the same discarding of the monetary-financial wrappings from the typical Asian economy, exposes, more clearly than before, the essential, systemic differences between both the American System and European economies, on the one side, and Asian economies on the other. That said, I now proceed accordingly. Several seemingly distinct features of that set of differences between European and Asian economies are now each being treated separately by me here, in order to show how these points, when combined as they actually interact, come together for a single, combined effect.

The roots of the Venetian system, whose proximate origins are ancient Rome, can be traced much further than that, by objective archeological studies, to as far back as the ruinous, predatory practice of usury in ancient Mesopotamia, where those practices led, repeatedly, to the collapse of the "bow tenure" agricultural system of lower Mesopotamia, practices also associated with the influence of the international "loan-sharking" attributed to the Delphi Apollo cult.[23]

Although the exploration of pre-European origins of the ideas of South, Southeast, and East Asia, must take into account influences dating from a time prior to significant medieval and modern European influences existing in those parts of the planet, the overwhelming evidence respecting relevant modern influences, shows that the dominant impact of relevance for the economies of modern Asia and Africa today, has been the impact of the spread of the Venetian model of financial practices, by the European colonizers, into the modern establishment of the Iberian and Anglo-Dutch Liberal colonization in those regions. There are obvious specifically Asian cultural factors in shaping the way populations of these regions adapted to the impact of the European colonizers, but the effects of the modern financial practices introduced to those areas during the recent five centuries, the effects to which local cultures reacted, are, still today, predominantly the effects of the role of Anglo-Dutch Liberal usury, and its pathological,

physiocratic mentality, as the triumphant successor to the Portuguese and Spanish.

When we look at the known history of European civilization from the vantage-point of my original contributions to a science of physical economy, the following is clear.

In the case of the emergence of modern European civilization, our attention is focussed on an impulse for development, most readily traced from ancient Egypt's influence on the founding of a distinct, Classical current in Greek civilization, an impulse for development which ultimately emerged as an integral feature of the Fifteenth-Century establishment of the modern European nation-state. In the contrasted case of Asian culture as experienced today, we are dealing, most prominently, as I shall explain at relevant places in this chapter of the report, with effects of a case of rape perpetrated by the likes of the pirates of Venice.

In the struggle for progress which is principally internal to modern European civilization, the vector of struggle has been the effort of modern European physical economy to throw off the yoke of the ancient, predatory Venetian usurer, to throw off the yoke of the ancient Roman empires and their Venetian-Norman, medieval successor. In the instance of today's Asian cultures, the yearning for independence from the contemporary Venetian Party's yoke of (presently) predatory IMF/World Bank usury, impels cultures of Asia to seek to acquire the means of modern physical economy (e.g., nuclear power) as weapons for breaking the chains of Venery.

As Leibniz or Bernhard Riemann might wish to say, in comment on the distinction I have just emphasized: *although "agro-industrial development" is "agro-industrial development," whether in transatlantic European cultures, or Asian cultures, in comparing the two cases, we are confronted with a proposition in* Analysis Situs.[24] *The same words, "agro-industrial development," applicable to both situations, have an essentially different functional significance in each application.* My emphasis on the relevance of *Analysis Situs* is, as I shall show, unignorably crucial for understanding the actual, functional relationship between Transatlantic and Asian/African cultures today. One, *the economic*

---

23. Archeological studies of the revived use of clay tablets in trade between Mesopotamia and the pre-dark-age, iron-weapons culture of the Hittites, gives us insight into what is initially the astonishing modernity of financial practices dating from 1600-1400 B.C. A study of the site of the Delphi Temple affords mute testimony to the connection between the Apollo cult and the ancient "loan-sharking" in the Mediterranean which played a crucial part in the processes leading into and from the Peloponnesian War and its sequelae. In turn, archeological studies bearing upon the calculable extent of so-called "Harrapan" culture during the period of a wetter climate, and a time when continental coastlines were more extended, ocean levels lower, and with cities which now remain as fossils on ancient, now-sunken coastlines, force us to abandon the quaint delusions of Nineteenth-Century British diggers making a mess of mountains of precious archeological relics (e.g., cuneiform tablets), in their zeal to become the first to turn up the exact street address for Abraham in Ur. The connection, referenced by Herodotus, between the Dravidian-language-group maritime culture which settled Sumer, and other parts of what we call the "Near East," must be studied more carefully before drawing definite conclusions about the origins of usury and other matters of ancient lower Mesopotamian practices. My own original discoveries in the field of a science of physical economy, date from work of the 1948-1953 interval. However, in the effort to test those discoveries' application to the study of prehistoric and related cultures, I concentrated considerable attention on the obvious role of transoceanic cultures in the development of riparian cultures during the period after the great melt of the last glaciation of much of the Northern Hemisphere's land-mass. Later work showed that close study of ancient systems of astronomy, including, notably, Egypt and ancient China, is of crucial importance for achieving a deeper understanding of the roots of sundry streams of Asian cultures. Appropriate references, touching on this, will appear in portions of the text below.

24. See *G.W. Leibniz: Philosophical Papers and Letters,* Leroy E. Loemker, ed. (Dodrecht: Kluwer Academic Publishers, 1989), pp. 248-262. Bernhard Riemann, *Theorie der Abel'schen Functionen*, in *Riemanns gesammelte mathematische Werke*, H. Weber, ed. (New York: Dover Reprint edition, 1953) pp. 88-144.

The German-designed Transrapid maglev train in Shanghai, China. "The most successful forms of European technology of economic development arrive in Asia as very much an immigrant into a land which is not quite certain as to whether you, the European, should really be welcomed, or not."

development of modern European civilization, comes from that culture; the other, modern economic development in Asia, for example, and also the lack of it, has been introduced to the culture chiefly from outside, without any competent consideration of the ironies of this crucial problem in Analysis Situs.

In my sometimes off-and-on experience with Asian culture since 1945-46, one can not step from the U.S.A., or Europe, inside the proverbial doorway of Asia, without being confronted with a powerfully emotional sense of the difference between those two situations, from reflections on discussions with one's conversation-partner there. In Asia, even among persons with what might be termed a "strong" basis in European knowledge, there is a difference which only a dull-witted product of European culture could overlook.

The best way to locate the source of the uneasiness a sensible person of European culture experiences, each time he or she steps freshly into an Asian cultural setting, is to bring the discussion to matters bearing upon the technological side of modern industrial and related development of any Asian economy considered as a whole. *The most successful forms of European technology of economic development arrive in Asia as very much an immigrant into a land which is not quite certain as to whether you, the European, should really be welcomed, or not.*[25]

____

25. As he advised U.S. President John F. Kennedy, General of the

I am sensitive to that, but I have long since ceased to worry myself about it in my dealings with the matter. My approach to the matter is to proceed from a higher vantage-point than either European or Asian culture, to seek *to stand on the platform of what I foresee as the necessary emergence of a specifically Eurasian culture,* the culture we must build up, shall we say, "a planetary culture," through efforts premised on an understanding of the fact that that must be our mission. That is the viewpoint which I hope I will be able to put across, at least in a preliminary way, in the course of this report.

We shall return to that matter at the appropriate point in this report. Now, in order to clarify the problem in *Analysis Situs* referred to just above, we must take a detour. Before we return to that point, we must first continue by returning our attention, for a time, to the American System, its impact on world development, and its crucial advantage over Europe.

The European Roots

The principled advantage of the American System is fairly summed up as follows:

The modern sovereign nation-state was born in Europe out of a long history of opposition to the oligarchical dogma of the Olympian Zeus, an opposition which is, most emphatically, a heritage of the current of such opposition expressed at Athens. That is the opposition which is associated most closely with Solon, Socrates, and Plato, which promoted that aspect of the human individual, the human immortal soul, which uniquely distinguishes man from ape.

This heritage, which is embraced by such Christian Apostles as, most notably, John and Paul, and also, otherwise, by Philo of Alexandria and others, locates the human identity, the immortal soul of the human individual, as Socrates and Plato define it, in those creative powers of the individual human mind, the power of Socratic-Platonic hypothesis, which are categorically

____

Armies Douglas MacArthur understood this, strategically and otherwise. Robert McNamara and his fellow wild-eyed, rapacious utopians, clearly did not, and still do not today.

absent in the beasts. These are the immortal creative powers which we associate with that specific conception of science which we trace, in European culture, from the ancient Pythagorean's adoption of the Egyptian standard of *Sphaerics* (i.e., science as derived by Egypt from the foundations of discoveries in the field of physical astronomy) and of an anti-reductionist conception of music, such as that of J.S. Bach, as opposed to the pathetic, empiricist triviality of a Rameau.

The Renaissance's freeing of the mass of the population from the status, in practice, of human herded or hunted cattle, as by the teaching and related practice of the Classical Greek humanists, caused revolutionary advances in the productive powers of labor in modern Europe, as the effect of the application of those powers may be measured, physically, in terms of per-capita output per square kilometer of territory of a certain relative quality (hence, *potential relative population-density*). These powers are those which the Classical Greeks, such as the Pythagoreans, associate with that modern definition of a universal physical principle which is typified by Johannes Kepler's uniquely original discovery of a universal physical principle of gravitation. Today, these measurements or powers, as distinct from mere mathematical formulas, are best defined afresh, as I shall indicate in this report, in terms of Vernadsky's Riemannian definition of the Noösphere.

These measurements, as understood by the methods of Sphaerics adopted by the Pythagoreans, are key to the advantage of modern European science and its physical economy, over alternate forms of society. Considered physically, that is without taking money itself into account, they account for the great physical advantage of modern European civilization, as in the U.S.A. and leading nations of Europe, over other cultures, as this can be measured both per capita and per square kilometer.

The advantage of modern European culture, has been, essentially, that the promotion of the freedom and education of the individual, especially when combined with promotion of the Classical European modes of scientific and technological progress, and of Classical culture, increases the developed creative potential of the individual. A society which is organized to promote and employ that increase of the promotion and realization of the creative potential of virtually all of its members, has a necessary advantage, by a large margin, over a society which has a contrary, or simply different policy of practice. This method, as typified by the work of the Platonic Academy of Athens, through Eratosthenes and beyond, was the great advantage in method of modern European culture over what are typical as so-called ancient or medieval forms of European society.

Thus, the fall of the U.S.A., in particular, from the level it achieved and maintained over the 1933-1964 interval, was chiefly a result of a negation of those factors of both U.S. policy and cultural development which had been the essential drivers of the nation's role as the world's leading producer society, with the relatively highest standard of living. It was through the realized effect of the counterculture launched under the auspices of the Congress for Cultural Freedom, that the youth entering leading universities from the mid-1960s onward, degenerated morally and intellectually in ways merely typified in the extreme by "the rock-drug-sex youth-counterculture." This latter form of corruption of the so-called "Baby Boomer" generation, in both North America and Europe, led into the political transformation of those cultures into an increasingly parasitical character as a decadent culture of "bread and circuses," an "entertainment society," mimicking the decadence of Rome, following the Second Punic War, into a predatory parasite, with a culture of "bread and circuses" at home. The ration and extent of mass countercultural "entertainment," including gambling manias, in the U.S.A. and western Europe, is typical of the way in which moral degeneration leads into the kind of disastrous economic degeneration which the U.S.A. and Europe are enjoying today.

The pre-1964 advantage of European culture's long sweep, was rooted in what Plato's dialogues define as that principle of *hypothesis* which is the correlative of the Classical Greek notion of *powers*, which was so foolishly and crudely rejected by empiricists Francis Bacon's and Thomas Hobbes' contempt for Classical irony of a Shakespeare. This is the folly also expressed by black magic specialist Isaac Newton's silly "Hypotheses non fingo," as by the Bertrand Russell who, with his devotees such as Norbert Wiener and John von Neumann, made a vast, intellectually sterile, abiotic system out of denying the existence of that function in the human individual which distinguishes man from the ape: the denial, by all such fools, of what Vernadsky termed the Noösphere.

All of the actual relative achievements in the development of European civilization, have been products of the development of that faculty, the principle of hypothesis, the noëtic power which sets man above such self-professed apes as Thomas Huxley, Frederick Engels, and the empiricists, positivists, and existentialists, as also the ancient Greek reductionists.

Thus, the essential historical problem impeding the long sweep of the development of modern European society as we have known it, has been the suppression of the individual's power of successful hypothesizing, a suppression accomplished in more or less the way typified by French Liberal empiricist, and probable *Fronde* sympathizer, François Quesnay's bestial argument in support of a principle of black magic he named *laissez-faire*.

As the U.S.'s Frederick Douglass emphasized, the most direct way in which to be able to herd people as human cattle, is to suppress their right to hypothesize in the mode illustrated by Plato's dialogues. Induce people to limit their behavior to those of their faculties which efficiently approximate the mentality of herded cattle, and you oblige them to behave, and to see themselves as a kind of dumb cattle. You can not free a slave, or a victim of the habit of slavery, without freeing him from the effects of a cattle-prod-like conditioning, such as conditioning never to be caught behaving as anything better than human cattle. This brutalization of many Americans of African descent was enforced in continuing effects today by such means as the U.S. Southern slaveholder clique's declaration of a slave's literacy as in itself a capital offense, and, later, after Emancipation, by Liberal policies of education intended to avoid encouraging a descendant of slavery to aspire to rise above his or her assigned, menial station in life. (In today's U.S.A., the same kind of effect is secured, still, in other ways. The relevant form of functional cognitive illiteracy is rationalized, as under President George W. Bush, Jr., as "their culture.")

It was to the extent that modern European culture practiced the use of its Classical advantage, that it leaped ahead of those non-European cultures which did not make this shift in social and economic policies of practice. This can be illustrated handily by comparing the estimated, average relative physical productivities, per capita and per square kilometer, for Europe, with those for, for example, India and China. Compare life, thus, in Europe, for example, from the census of Charlemagne through the Fourteenth Century, with that of the area of India and China during comparable times. Then study the shift, comparing Europe with the area of today's India and China, in fairly estimatable relative values of productivity per capita and per square kilome-

ter, over the interval 1400-1964. Then, look back to the demographic and related decline of, first, Imperial Rome in the West, and, after that, in Byzantium.

Admittedly, we did not even begin to actually free the people generally from the status of human cattle, until the emergence of modern European culture in the Fifteenth-Century Renaissance; but, we intended to realize that goal; and, that intention, wherever it persisted, made the difference in the character of European culture as a whole. It is as if to say, that a single person in a culture, by being and acting so, may supply a characteristic which becomes part of that culture as a whole, even a redeeming part of a culture which might be predominantly brutish in every other way. It is as if to think, that for the sake of the existence and work of a single good man, God might withhold terrible, just punishment from an entire erring people.

We who fought, sometimes as lonely individuals, when others were too frightened to do so, for the morally necessary supremacy of the Classical human conception of man, as distinct from, and above other creatures, maintained that tradition over millennia. The goal has lived because so many among us have put their mortal lives at stake, such as the modern Reverend Martin Luther King, or, like Jeanne d'Arc, were burned alive at the stake, for that mission in service of future mankind. Indeed, her dedication to her mission, was the inspiration which stirred the conscience of the Council of the Church, and which inspired France to gain its freedom from the Norman oppressor. We have fought so, often at greater or relatively less risk, to keep that principle alive within in civilization. This immortal commitment, sanctified by the sacrifices, which many of so many generations have made on its behalf, has preserved this principle as a characteristic of European civilization. It not only makes the difference today; the continued existence of civilization now depends upon that legacy, absolutely.

So, we of the U.S.A., today, most of whom have done little lately as individuals for us to brag about, are still a special nation among nations, because of what the heroes who have sometimes led us, and those others who worked, or have often sacrificed, have done, to provide the world as a whole today, the unique gift which our republic represents, a republic by aid of which this planet might be saved from the presently onrushing menace of a prolonged dark age.

To preserve that principle embedded in the intention of our U.S. Declaration of Independence and the Pre-

"The germ of the idea of creating the United States was already implied in the thinking of the martyred Sir Thomas More, whose judicial murder, already, in and of itself, made a strong case for setting the founding of a durable form of republic on the opposite side of the Atlantic."

amble and Presidential system of our original Constitution, we have endured much evil. As I have already said above: Typical of the malicious opposition which we have had to fight, in defense of the Classical humanist principle, is the case of the Physiocratic dogma of France's Dr. François Quesnay, an explicit adversary of the Classical humanist principle, and implicitly an evil one.

Quesnay's argument for *laissez-faire* (which the similarly depraved Adam Smith plagiarized as "free trade") is premised on two leading assumptions. First, the superstition, that the profit of the estate is caused by magical properties attributable to the landlord's title, rather than the labor of the workers on that estate.[26]

Second, that the function of the workers is comparable to that of milk cows, whom one must feed sufficiently that they live and breed to produce meat and milk, but are permitted no other moral claim to a share of the income. Otherwise, the income of society is attributed to the proprietors' ownership and exploitation of pre-existing natural resources; the notion that man contributes qualitatively to maintaining and increasing such resources by human labor, is rejected.

This physiocratic delusion, of Quesnay, Turgot, and the Adam Smith who plagiarized them both, is the underlying assumption of both current fads of "environmentalism," globalization, and virtual slave-labor practices of the IMF/World Bank-dominated international monetary-financial system today. As the physical economy of the Americas and Europe, in particular, is being looted into a state of net negative physical growth at home, the world's financier oligarchs of today are occupied by an obsession with grabbing control over natural resources, such as petroleum and other mineral resources, as a basis for world rule for generations—or, better said, "degenerations"—to come. The great financial-derivatives speculation in grabbing such natural resources, and the accelerating rate of inflation in those commodities resulting from that pyramided financial speculation in titles to such assets, is not only a characteristic of recent trends in world markets, but is, in fact, a symptom, and, also, a leading contributing cause of the global system's presently onrushing early collapse.

Why, Only in Our United States

To identify the crucial point as simply as possible, as I have already implied, the germ of the idea of creating our United States was already implied in the thinking of the martyred Sir Thomas More, whose judicial murder, already, in and of itself, made a strong case for setting the founding of a durable form of republic on the opposite side of the Atlantic, a case so defined by the manner of his untimely, and most unjust death at the order of an insane monarch manipulated by a pack of Venetian scoundrels.[27] Indeed, there were most proba-

---

26. If one thinks Quesnay and Smith to be already more than bad enough, the arch-liberal Bernard Mandeville, of **The Fable of the Bees** notoriety, the satanic figure worshipped by von Hayek's and Milton Friedman's Mont Pelerin Society, is frankly disgusting. The rabidly Gnostic Mandeville insists upon what might be called "The Enron Principle," that good in the large is a derivative of wickedness in the small, that great riches of the few come from much stealing from many little people. The promotion of gambling as a substitute for productive industry, is an example of this disgusting dogma.

27. E.g., Francesco Zorzi (a.k.a. Giorgi), putative chief of the Venice intelligence service, and posted to England to operate under the cover of a marriage counsellor to King Henry VIII; Cardinal Pole, Plantagenet pretender to the throne of England, and Venice agent; Thomas Cromwell, Venice-trained agent. The first implication of that operation, was

bly similar thoughts by Miles Standish nearly a century later, and that, certainly, was the line of thinking of the leaders of the founding and development of that Massachusetts Bay Colony which was to become the seed-kernel for the creation of our U.S.A.

In effect, during the interval 1763-66, Benjamin Franklin and his circles returned to the implied American concern of Sir Thomas More. The question posed from the mid-Seventeenth-Century onwards, was, implicitly: Was it necessary for Americans to go so far in resisting the recently spawned British Empire, as to think of a war-like break, to independence, from that cruel empire? The answer, as experience affirmed that view, was that not only was the revolutionary independence of the English colonies in North America justified, as the U.S. Declaration of Independence avows; it was necessary for the sake of the liberation of Europe's nations from the ultimately fatal corruption of which Europe could not otherwise cure itself. The creation of our new republic must be the adoption of the best from Europe, but the best freed from the fatal corruption of the existing, institutionalized culture of Europe.

This was implicitly the same corroborating observation made by Friedrich Schiller in viewing the horrors of the French Revolution: A great historic opportunity had been lost, because the moment had found a people morally too small-minded to seize that long-awaited opportunity when it had been presented. What should have happened in France in 1789, was realized by the role of the U.S.A. under President Franklin Roosevelt. Roosevelt led in freeing a Europe which had brought the blight of the Jacobin Terror and Napoleon upon itself earlier, and fascism more recently, through its own continuing cultural-political corruption, its failure to have broken with the quasi-feudal cultural legacy of the Anglo-Dutch Liberal and some even earlier traditions, such as the Habsburg legacy.

Today, the same logic says: "We must free our U.S.A. from its present seizure by the infection of a fatal corruption like that which afflicted Europe in the two so-called 'world wars' and rise of fascism in the past, that we might, once again, take that action which would save our republic from its own present lunacy, while also saving Europe from its own present folly."

Today, even what a European view may see as the massive corruption of the virtually self-bankrupted U.S.A., has not changed that question in any essential way. As I have emphasized repeatedly earlier in this present report, Europe may see the corruption of today's U.S.A., but Europe is not prepared to assume the responsibility for the specific kind of measures through which it might tend to assume the kind of leadership role which the history of the U.S. requires it to play in the world today.

For example: At this moment of writing, there are, in fact, two strategic polarities of the planet which will play a dominant, virtually decisive role in determining the direction which world history may take at the present juncture. One is typified by the attack on Social Security, by the present Bush Administration, from inside the U.S.A. This is an issue which is echoed in similar institutional forms in western Europe, and in similar ways throughout central and south America. The outcome of this fight over the privatization of Social Security will tend to determine whether a U.S. under President George W. Bush goes fascist, or not, and that soon. The other polarity is the keystone role of Russia in the Eurasia context as a whole, as this is typified by the network of collaboration centered around the nest of Russia-India-China treaty relations. It is the intersection of these two global polarities, which will define the phase-spaces in which all other significant issues of the planet as a whole are resolved strategically.

For example: The likelihood is that President George W. Bush could lose his mad dash for early privatization of Social Security. It is the single issue on the table now which would be most likely to sink Bush politically in the quickest time. If the U.S.A. were to go in that direction, this would mean the rapid spread of already-suppurating tendencies for austerity-cum-fascist regimes throughout much of the world. If, as is at least likely, Bush is defeated on this, a positive turn in the strategic situation becomes possible, as distinct from the immediate alternative, in which the political health of the U.S., and therefore the planet, is doubtful.

For example: The state of mind around the Bush Presidency at this time, is that an alarming ration of voters do say "Yes!" to the test question: "Do you accept George Bush as your personal Lord and Savior?"

---

to incite a quarrel between the Spanish Hapsburgs and England, with a Spain which had already chosen France as the principal target of its murderous feuding. In the end, the operation played into the hands of what was to become, later in that century, the new virtual tyrant of Venice, "new party" head Paolo Sarpi, who personally prepared the way for the 1618-1648 Thirty Years' War, and thus orchestrated the foundations of the Anglo-Dutch Liberal Venetian Party's emergence as what became Shelburne lackey Gibbon's new, Anglo-Dutch Liberal model for a Roman Empire. Shades of the Democratic Party of Athens, et al. (i.e., the Sophists) in the Peloponnesian War.

In this setting, with such a healthy quality of support for the Bush Presidency and the role of pro-fascist, lunatic circles within the Democratic Party, around Zbigniew Brzezinski, on a strategic collision-course over the Ukraine election and related matters, the corresponding shift in the strategic posture of Russia's President V. Putin, especially the strategic emphasis on a Eurasian cooperation bloc centered around cooperation among Russia, India, and China, is the pivotal counter to the Bush Administration's global posture. Any matter which does not fold into that U.S.-Russia complex, is either of marginal relevance, or is being misdefined by lack of a competent strategic focus.

This Washington-Moscow pivot of the presently rising tempo of global strategic confrontation and related developments, affirms, despite the decadence of the U.S. political and economic institutions, the continuing crucial role of the U.S. in determining the options for survival or breakdown of present world civilization.

That said, as a matter of needed qualification of the argument, resume the development of the historical point.

That, as observed from the parapet of the experience of modern European history, takes us now to the most profound of the questions posed by consideration of the crisis of Asian culture today. The subject now, therefore, is the nature and indispensable role of national sovereignty.

Throwing out the rubbish is an essential part of progress. The expression, "Go someplace else to get a fresh start," often expresses a drunk's, perhaps George W. Bush, Jr.'s ("I have been thrown out of far better joints than this one!") or other neurotic's flight from reality; but, sometimes it reflects a profound truth. Such was the intent, as expressed by Cardinal Nicholas of Cusa, behind the launching of the great voyages of discovery which, among not-unintended effects, produced the U.S.A.

The typical neurotic problem of cultures, as much as individual persons, is that the individual's, or nation's collective mind is usually like a fishbowl. Thoughts swim within a fishbowl-like container, whose walls are composed of a blend of real, and false assumptions which exert axiomatic authority over the opinions of the inmate. Therefore, the actions of the subject persons are limited to moving among the available destinations located within the confinement of that ideological fishbowl.

When the Venetian resurgence against the great ecumenical Council of Florence, used the flanking strategy of promoting the Ottoman conquest of Constantinople as the leading initiative for an attempt to destroy the Fifteenth-Century Renaissance, Cusa had responded with his proposal for transoceanic, globe-spanning voyages of exploration, to seek new partners abroad for the global intention of the great ecumenical mission of the Renaissance effort. There were several profound principles expressed in this way; one, which seems to have passed through the Renaissance mind of Sir Thomas More, is most relevant for consideration as a general principle of global strategy for today.

As I have just emphasized, the process leading into the creation of the U.S. Federal Constitutional republic, has two unique features:

First, as the case of Cusa's, and also Sir Thomas More's role in launching the program which led into the creation of the U.S. illustrates the point: The idea of developing an extension, in foreign continents, of the best features of a European civilization conceived by the Italy-centered Renaissance, was not a scheme for abandoning the troublesome Europe of that time, but part of a program for outflanking the problems of Europe, by developing the external leverage of new fraternal relations developed in places which were at a convenient distance from Europe at that time.

Second, as typified by the role of leadership, typified by the Winthrops and the Mathers, the early explorers and settlers of North America found in that awesomely difficult wilderness, an excellent place from which to build up an extension of the best features of European culture, a place which could develop relatively free of those existing, stubbornly tragic features of Europe's life and customs up to that time. This place, especially a North America relatively free of the lunacy which the Habsburg gang had left as a legacy to the South, offered an opportunity for action which might overcome the deadly cultural sicknesses which persisted inside Europe as baggage carried forward from the past. As my late friend and historian H. Graham Lowry emphasized in his ***How the Nation was Won***,[28] the Winthrop family which founded the Massachusetts Bay Colony, especially prior to 1688-1689, represented precisely those qualities of leadership which Sir Thomas More would have admired for such a project.

From the Seventeenth-Century beginning of the de-

---

28. (Washington, D.C.: Executive Intelligence Review, 1987).

velopment of what later became the U.S.A., there was no significant intention among the American colonists to break with the British monarchy itself. The leaders among the colonists understood that their principal enemy in England was what William of Orange and his Anglo-Dutch India Company represented. The colonists found themselves in a quarrel with the Liberal Parliament of Walpole and his successors, but hoped, as the leadership role of Benjamin Franklin expresses this most clearly, that the English monarch might keep the paws of William of Orange's and Marlborough's Venetian Party off the autonomous subjects of the King in North America. It was as the English monarchs themselves showed themselves, more and more, to be creatures of the Venetian Party's India Company, that the Americans were driven reluctantly to see the break as unavoidable.

The same pattern showed itself in the case of U.S. relations with Eighteenth-Century France, as a tragic element in the role of the Marquis de Lafayette's conflict between loyalties to his cause and his King, shows this. So, President George Washington understood, and warned against further search for "entangling alliances" in the Europe of that time.

So, back in Europe, not only in England, but in general, the relevant leaders there understood quite clearly that the chief immediate threat to any attempt to better European life came from the predatory, Venice-centered financier oligarchy which had led Europe into the nightmare of the Fourteenth-Century New Dark Age, a time in which half of the parishes of Europe virtually evaporated, and there had been a net loss of population of an estimated one-third of the total population. In 1648, as the great peace Treaty of Westphalia finally brought to an end a period of religious persecutions and wars unleashed beginning 1492, and once the emerging power of the new Venetian Party, the Anglo-Dutch Liberal power, was pushing Europe into another round of the kinds of troubles which Venice had represented since about A.D. 1000, the idea arose of using the Americas, particularly North America, as a base from which efforts to outflank the newly emerging menace might be prepared and launched by people who had settled in North America from Europe.

The successive waves of migration, from Europe into North America, the U.S.A. most emphatically, expressed a corresponding principle. The masses fled the apparently hopelessly stubborn corruption of Europe, not because they sought to break with the mother-culture with which they had been reared, but because they saw an otherwise poor future for the good products of their culture in Europe itself.

Behind all this, there is a deeper principle, to which we shall return after preparing the ground for that by focussing, now, on some essential points about what Alexander Hamilton and others of that and later times called "the American System."

'The American System'

In the midst of what became known as the Seven Years' War, the British East India Company had set into motion, and orchestrated operations intended to undermine, and ultimately to destroy all among the rival powers of continental Europe, the Company's most feared, and therefore most hated target, was a growing network from among the greatest thinkers of Europe at that time, a network which extended to the leading North American scientist and political figure of that time, Benjamin Franklin.

Among the pivotal European influences targetted by the Anglo-Dutch Liberal's transatlantic project was one Abraham Kästner, a leading follower of Gottfried Leibniz, a leading mathematician in the field of Leibniz's work, a defender of the work of Johann Sebastian Bach, and a person of special political influence among the circles of the Classical humanist culture, such as the circles of Gotthold Lessing and Moses Mendelssohn, arising in Germany at that time. Through this and related channels, relevant works of Leibniz, including his attack on John Locke in Leibniz's *New Essays on Human Understanding,* exerted a profound influence on shaping the world-outlook and philosophy of law of the founding of the U.S.A.

Among these European connections targetted by the London-centered Liberal gang, were the circles around Franklin which had adopted Leibniz's anti-Locke principle, the pursuit of happiness, as the central positive Constitutional principle of the 1776 U.S. Declaration of Independence. In this context, Leibniz's science of physical economy became the scientific basis for what U.S. Treasury Secretary Alexander Hamilton was to identify prominently as the *American System of political-economy.*

Leibniz's science of physical economy, which he developed over the interval 1671-1716, represented the original discovery of a science of physical economy, the first and only form of an actual science of economics developed in Europe up to that time. No competent

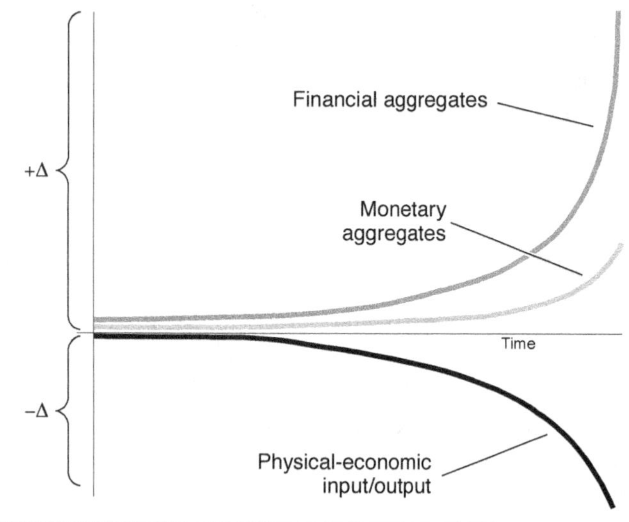

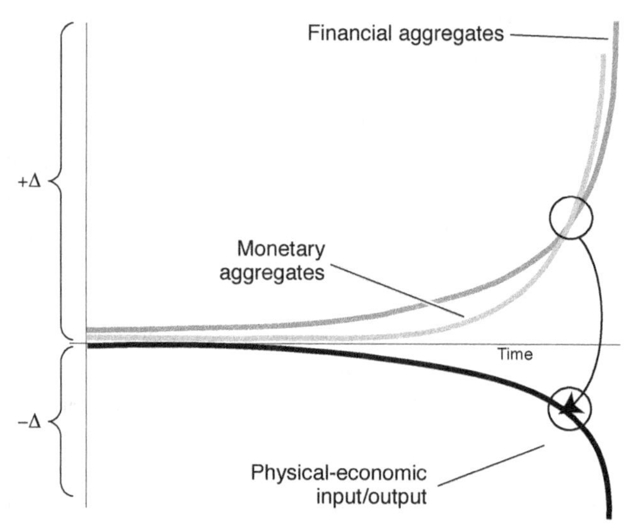

LaRouche's "triple curve" heuristic diagrams show the cannibalization of the physical economy, by the hyperbolic growth of monetary and financial aggregates. In the figure on the right, the growth of monetary aggregates overtakes financial aggregates, leading to hyperinflation—a situation we are beginning to see today.

understanding of any of the leading problems of culture identified here so far, could be defined and addressed in a way which matches the requirements of physical science, on any different basis than Leibniz's founding of economic science in his work on this subject during that interval. What is called "economics" in most universities and related professional institutions today, is essentially methods of accounting, methods which have no connection whatsoever with a body of science in the sense of the use of the term "physical science."

For example, since 1971-1972, the U.S. economy has been operating under a doctrine which is named by some of its leading authors as a policy of "controlled disintegration of the economy." The radically inflationary interest-rate shock introduced, in October-November 1979, by newly appointed Federal Reserve Chairman Paul Volcker, is an example of this policy promulgated by the followers of Carter Administration National Security Advisor Zbigniew Brzezinski as the long-range program of the Brzezinski-led Trilateral Commission. In principle, that had also been the pre-Carter Administration policy of a Nixon Administration group headed by George Shultz, Paul Volcker, and Henry A. Kissinger. In physical terms, the U.S. economy has been collapsing consistently over the interval 1971-2004; however, thanks to the combined kind graces of inflation and of the flagrantly fraudulent reporting of statistics by the Federal Reserve System and certain Federal government agencies, your average American dupe came to believe, falsely, that the economy has been growing, despite a few set-backs here and there, a deluded belief which has been continued during most of this period.

All the while, as my Triple Curve pedagogies [**Figures 3a and 3b**] have illustrated this fact consistently, since their first general publication in 1996, the U.S. physical economy not only did plunge into what I had forecast as a deep stock-market crash, in October 1987, from whose permanent effects it never recovered structurally; but, the consistent trend since that crash, as before, has been an accelerating expansion of monetary and financial circulation, with, also, an accelerating decline in net physical output per capita. Meanwhile, the majority of a credulous upper twenty percentile of the population, reads most glowing reports of the rate of expansion of monetary-supply and selected financial market indices, and seems not to recognize the consistent collapse of the rates of net national physical output per capita and per square kilometer.

For example, an international monetary-financial

crisis was already in progress during 1995-1996, but the governments and money-managers, combined, were able to dump the burden of the 1997 collapse, with George Soros's help, on the Asian markets, and to dump the burden of the ensuing August-September 1998 crisis on the speculative market in Russian GKO bonds, all as a result of a wild-eyed swindle of about everyone, including themselves, by a bevy of leading hedge-fund speculators.

Two observations are to be made on account of that and comparable examples.

First, although the use of monetary-financial trickery is a tactic which has often succeeded in postponing the appearance in monetary-financial markets, of a collapse already underway in the physical (real) economy, the conditioning of relevant leading governmental and other institutions into reading financial accounting reports, rather than seeing physical facts of the real situation, allows governments and others to use inflation as a mask to postpone the public recognition of even a severe economic decline which has already occurred, to postpone that recognition for a period of years or longer after the collapse has already occurred in the physical base of the economy.

Second, there are the combined factors of the accelerating trend toward globalization, and the lowering of the level of sanity of the population, through the shift from a producer economy to a debt-as-money, pleasure-seekers' economy. This tactic uses the misleading "wealth effect" of a "plastic" credit-economy in promoting the loss of net savings in a bank, the loss of conditions of stable currency to cost-of-living correlations, to promote a thus-deluded general population's tendency to mistake short-term, high-premium debt-slavery for a satisfying level of income. That prolonged swindle, over a generation, has produced two adult generations of our post-World War II population, who, increasingly, have lost their connection to our population's former practical sense of the functional connection among production, income, debt, and consumption.

Even before that recent three decades or so of a rising epidemic of mass-insanity took over, what was usually mistaken by misled popular opinion for "economics," was, and remains a branch of accounting, not science. What is peddled, in universities and elsewhere, under the label of economics, was developed by the British East India Company after the U.S. Declaration of Independence was adopted, and was developed at that time, and later, as the British financier oligarchy's

effort to develop a doctrine of political-economy intended to block out international attention to the Leibniz-based American System of political-economy. Liberals' London turned to the circles of Lord Shelburne's Jeremy Bentham to organize the British East India Company's Haileybury school's program in political economy, from which all of what may be termed fairly "the usual suspects" of British political-economy, as taught still today, are derived.

I have treated the issues posed by this contrast in locations published earlier. Here, in this present report, I confine our attention to those points which are of essential relevance to, firstly, the contrasts among American System physical-economy and European monetarist systems, and secondly, the root of the relevant cultural differences between American and European culture, on the one side, and Asian culture, the other. On this account, in order to place the needed, correct emphasis on physical economy, rather than intrinsically deceptive monetary-financial "wealth effects," I have situated the arguments for that American System which was derived from Leibniz's discovery of a science of physical economy against the backdrop of Vernadsky's notion of the Noösphere.

Admittedly, the names and trick accessories of the currently taught doctrines change, as Wall Street finance's reform of automobile marketing imitated the design-change policies of New York's Seventh Avenue garment district. Today's new fashions in economics doctrine should remind us of a half-naked skeleton draped in scanty rags, marching—to a bony, rhythmical clack, clack, clack—down the Milan fashion-parade line-up today. Essentially, in both cases, there has been relatively minimal improvement, if any, either in function, or in taste. Give us our factories back, and feed and clothe those poor, starving, shivering girls, now that Winter is coming on!

In their attempts to defame and undermine that pro-Leibnizian American System of political-economy which we associate with the names of Franklin, Alexander Hamilton, the Careys, Frederick List, Abraham Lincoln, and President Franklin Roosevelt today, the Anglo-Dutch Liberal gang proceeded with their knowledge, from the inside of their culture itself, that the American System of political-economy was the greatest imaginable long-term threat to Lord Shelburne's plan for a global, new Roman Empire based in London. So, they proceeded against Franklin and the American System, just as those Liberals had defamed what they feared as the work of Leibniz, because they knew it was absolutely superior to, and a danger to the authority of empiricism.

The Liberals' preferred tactical method is, to destroy whatever it fears to be superior to its system, by, first, fraudulently defaming that target, as those Liberals have spent more time and energy, especially during the recent thirty years, in continuing fraudulent defamations against me personally than any other living intellectual figure they have targetted on this planet. Those Liberals never waste much effort in prolonged defaming of what they do not recognize as both dangerously truthful and deadly to their special strategic interests. In short, they lie Liberally, sometimes, very Liberally.

The entirety of the Anglo-Dutch Liberal system in statecraft in general, and economy in particular, was and remains a vast hoax, a hoax now in the process of crashing down around the world's ears, including those of the legendary British Twiggy's successors, the poor, shivering, super-skinny girls in Milan today.

To rescue this present civilization from its threatened self-inflicted doom, the standpoint from which a competent modern science will address physical science, Classical culture, and political-economy, all in a common way, is that ancient Classical Greek scientific method associated with, as I have already emphasized earlier in this report, the pre-Aristotle scientific conceptions and methods of Thales, the Pythagoreans, and Plato. From this ancient standpoint, on which the launching of modern European experimental science was premised, science expressed in a unified way the conception of the special nature of the human being, as distinct from and absolutely superior to all other known forms of living beings.

What I have just said appears to put the emphasis on physical values. It does in large degree, but the functional aspects of authentically Classical forms of artistic composition, are also physical, as I shall emphasize that important point, in passing, in this present report.

The greatest enemy of global civilization today, is not so much the Anglo-Dutch Liberal system of economy itself, as the misleading ideology, respecting the nature of science in particular, and truth in general, which had been induced in official and popular currents of opinion as a part of the process of "brainwashing" society into accepting the so-called "philosophy" of Big Brother's Liberal system. Therefore, it is to that root of the corruption, as in science and related areas, that we must now turn our attention on the subject of the relationship between science and culture.

The central theme of this ancient, and modern physical science, is the conception of *powers*, as the Pythagoreans and others adopted this conception from the methods of Egyptian physical astronomy, known as *Sphaerics*. This conception is replicated in a unique and exemplary way for astronomy, by the work of the ancient Aristarchus and Eratosthenes, and the discovery of universal gravitation by the Johannes Kepler from whose pioneering work all competent modern physical science was either derived or otherwise inspired.

Kepler's work, premised, as he insisted, on the guidance of predecessors such as Cardinal Nicholas of Cusa, Luca Pacioli, and Leonardo da Vinci, was the foundation for all competent modern physical astronomy, and for the offshoots of his work in astronomy such as the original discovery of a universal infinitesimal calculus by Leibniz, and the mastery of the implications of elliptical functions by Carl Gauss, Bernhard Riemann, and others. What is called the elementarily geometric method of Kepler's discovery of universal gravitation, and is also the way in which Leibniz derived a calculus and the related universal principle of physical least action, is perfectly consistent with the notion of *Sphaerics* as known from the work of those relevant pre-Aristotle Greek scientists such as Thales, the Pythagoreans, and Plato.

The universal physical principles consistent with both the ancient and modern conceptions of Sphaerics are termed *powers,* in English-language usage. But, the methods of those scientists are not consistent with the empiricist notions of algebraic types of representation of that misleading mathematical form of expression of the principles of physics prescribed in the work of Galileo, and the Newtonians such as d'Alembert, Euler, Lagrange, Cauchy, Clausius, Helmholtz, et al.

With the return by Vernadsky, in his work on the Noösphere, fully to the Classical, geometric method of the Classical, pre-Aristotle Greek scientists in the Pythagorean-Platonic tradition, we have today, in the implications of Vernadsky's work, the desired "common language" of the type of experimental method required for addressing more efficiently those issues of economy and culture posed in this present report.

As I shall emphasize, this notion of powers is applicable not only to subject-matters associatable with the domain of physical science, but also those aspects of social processes which are apotheosized in the form of principles of Classical artistic composition. Such are

The pro-Leibnizian American System of political-economy is associated with the work of Benjamin Franklin (above), Alexander Hamilton (right), and Abraham Lincoln (far right). The Anglo-Dutch Liberals fought to destroy all three, because they knew the American System was absolutely superior to, and a danger to the authority of empiricism.

EIRNS/Stuart Lewis

Library of Congress

the minimum scientific requirements for sorting out the three categories of global, economy-significant cultural problems addressed in this report.

For example, consider the following summary of that point, this time from the vantage-point of the cultural implications of the Alexander Hamilton definition of the principles of development under the American System of political-economy. As in this present report, I premise the argument upon the presentation of a notion of a universal physical principle, as such a principle must be properly defined from the standpoint of the Classical notion of *powers*. I interpolate a fresh restatement of the definition of powers as applied to this purpose. At this point, I provide the reader a glossary of some of the most essential concepts which form an indispensable part of the vocabulary of economic management practice in general, and of the government of a progressive form of sovereign nation-state republic most emphatically. I begin with the concept of "power."

Define 'Power'

The notion of a *power*, as associated with the method of the Pythagoreans and Plato, is inseparable from the notion of the difference between a higher ape and a human being. The distinctions and their immediate implications may be summarized as follows.

The notion of a *power*, in the sense that the Pythagoreans, for example, employ that term as a by-product of the practice of astronomy (e.g., *Sphaerics*), expresses a peculiarity of that behavioral potential of the developable human being which sets man apart from, and absolutely above the higher apes. That concept of *power* is defined, briefly, in the following way.

Our sense-perceptions are not a direct representation of the reality we are experiencing. Our sense-organs are part of our biological apparatus, which present to our living, cognitive system, that apparatus's reaction to stimulus by the real world. It is those reactions which our sense-organs report, rather than the real world, which stimulate us initially. The basis for what the socially developed individual mind regards as sense-perceptions, is, at best, at its best, the mind's reading of an effect on our biological sense-organs' encounter with the world around us. We are, thus, given, not an answer, but, rather, a question which we must solve. In other words, what we consider our sense-perceptions of the world outside our skins, and the pain and pleasure within, are shadows which reality casts upon our merely mortal, biological sense-apparatus.

As Plato illustrates this point in his ***Republic***, and the Apostle Paul in ***I Corinthians*** 13, what we think we have seen are comparable to the shadows which a fire-light might cast on the irregular surface of the wall of the interior of a cave.

To know the real world around us, we must take another step, lest we mistake sense-perceptions for that which has prompted the sense-perception, lest we mistake the footprint for the foot. We must discover, by the aid of the same methods used to discover truth in experimental physical science, what the objects are which have cast those shadows.

This search for the real meaning hidden behind those shadows which we call sense-perceptions, leads human beings to two distinctly different types of discoveries, as follows.

The first type of problem is: Once we have been born, we must begin to make sense of that stream of sense-perceptions which seems to pour in from the world around the infant. Gradually, by aid of coordinating the streams of evidence supplied by the senses, the infant's mind transforms those streams into a world of perceived sensory objects. These sensory objects are then "seen" by the mind in the form of a product of that complex process of "digestion" of sensory streams. In this form, they are actual mental objects, objects which the mind creates in the individual's effort to gain control over the sensory world around him.

For example, the healthy mind of the infant does not simply see the parent as a kind of mathematical image projected on a digital computer's screen. The infant takes the combined experience obtained through the work of all of the senses, to distinguish objects which the child comes to identify with what he, or she later names as a functional relationship of that child to "mother," "father," and so on. In the case of the sanely functioning mind, the solution is not simply a product of each isolated type of repeated experience. It is the whole universe of the experience of the child's mind which is operating in each and all particular matters. In the sane child, the image of the parent as the parent might appear in any, and every situation, is inseparable from that idea of the parent, an idea of a relationship defined in terms of not merely sense-experience, but the values associated with the sense of relationship to the object, in which the sense of the relationship is primary, and the subject, and the related experiences predicates. One comes to know not only the idea of mother, but to associate that idea with a name which is used by people to address, or to refer to that mother.

However, with human individuals, rather than, for example, great apes, there is another aspect to this business of perceiving functional relationships among objects synthesized from streams of sensations. The human mind is also able to discover another class of objects, a class of objects which includes what we call "universal physical principles."

The only part of the class of mental objects we should refer to as "universal physical principles" which we need consider for the aims of this report on the challenge of Eurasian culture, are mental objects, objects which do not occur as sense-objects, mental objects which physical science puts into the class of the universal physical principles defined by methods of crucial experiments.[29] This class of principles is typified by the experimental methods employed by Johannes Kepler to prove his uniquely original discovery of a principle of universal gravitation. [See **Figures 4a and 4b**, and animations at www.larouchepac.com They are also objects of the type which empiricists class, falsely, as mathematically "imaginary," which appear in that process of a continuous process in constructive geometry which Plato's friend, the ancient Archytas, used to solve the problem of doubling a cube by a continuous process of purely geometric construction. [See **Figure 5**, and animations at www.schillerinstitute.org]

The processes by which discoveries of universal physical principles are generated, are of a qualitatively (i.e., absolutely) higher order of species than the processes of perception-conception which appear in the animals. They are of the class which Vernadsky associates with the distinction of the Noösphere from the Bio-

---

29. By this time, some of the readers of this report will have found themselves confronted by a lurking question to which I can give effective answer only at a slightly later point in this report as a whole. If, as we must insist, the cognitive behavior of the human mind, which Riemann and others have associated with a special significance for the German term *Geistesmasse*, poses the question: How can a merely living specimen of the Biosphere actually know concepts which lie within the Noösphere? Obviously, we do not know the latter concepts as products of the same biology applicable to non-human living beings; they exist in fact, in that of us which belongs within the domain of the Noösphere, and in terms of the shadows which the Noösphere casts upon the Biosphere, the effects produced by the function of the Noösphere upon the lower realm, the Biosphere. We know that which casts the shadows, by the effect which it casts. That understanding, and functional approach, is, in fact, the essence of the Platonic dialectical method. Only the human mind can understand the noëtic processes of the human mind.

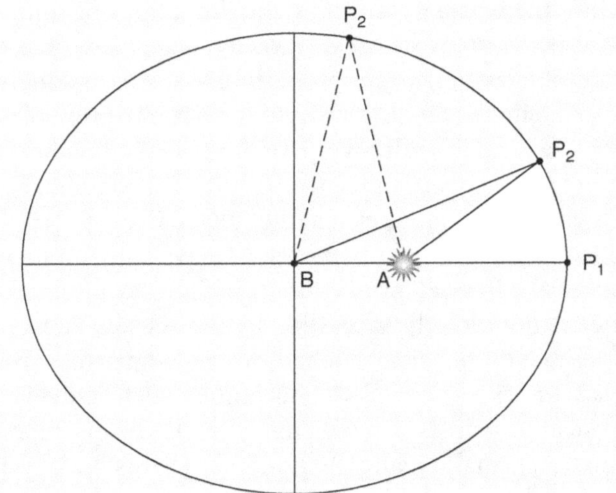

Kepler's elliptical orbit hypothesis. Here, length P2B is not constant, but constantly changing at a changing rate. What lawful process now underlies the generation of swept-out areas?

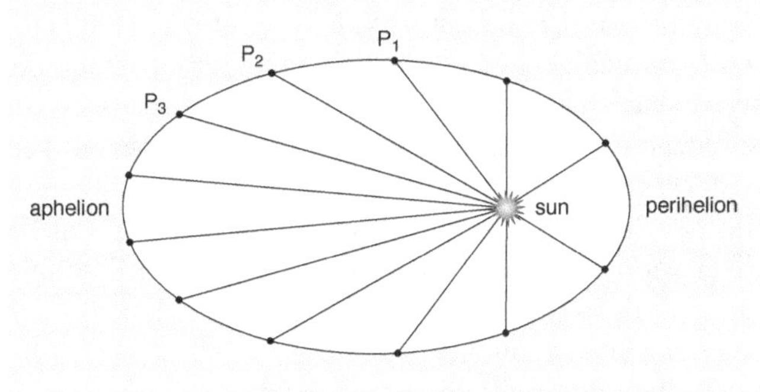

Kepler's constraint for motion on an elliptical orbit. The ratios of elapsed times are proportional to the ratios of swept-out areas. In equal time intervals, therefore, the areas of the curvilinear sectors swept out by the planet, will be equal—even though the curvilinear distances traversed on the orbit are constantly changing. In the region about perihelion, nearest the sun, the planet moves fastest, covering the greatest orbital distance; whereas, at aphelion, farthest from the sun, it moves most slowly, covering the least distance. This constraint is known as Kepler's "area law," later referred to as his "Second Law."

Archytas' Construction for Doubling of the Cube

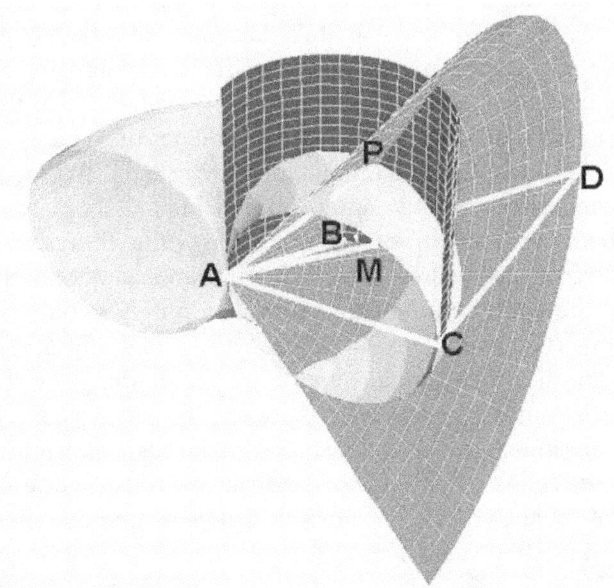

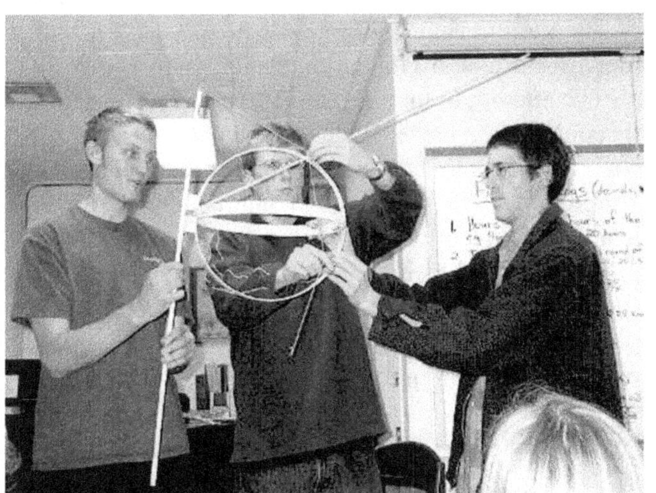

Archytas' solution to the Delian paradox typifies the work of pre-Euclidean, physical, constructive geometry. Here, members of the LaRouche Youth Movement have built a pedagogical device to demonstrate his solution, which creates a cone, a torus, and a cylinder in order to find the geometric means between two magnitudes—AC and AB in the drawing.

sphere. The point being developed here on that account, requires a brief historical survey of the following bench-marks of relevant scientific progress from ancient to modern times.

This class of principles which we know today as universal physical principles of experimental methods, became known to the ancient Greek science of such figures as Thales, the Pythagoreans, Plato, the Aristarchus of Samos who proved experimentally, more than a century after the death of Plato, that the Earth orbits the Sun, and the Eratosthenes who measured the circumference of the Earth, prior to 200 B.C., by comparing the shadows cast by sunlight at two proximate points, on a North-South line, in Egypt. Eratosthenes, who also measured the distance from Alexandria, Egypt, to Rome, Italy, by "deep well" astronomical methods, was a leading member of Plato's Academy of Athens, although he spent most of his adult life as a leading figure of the Egypt of his time. The same Eratosthenes was the correspondent of the famous Archimedes of Syracuse.

Another figure from ancient Greece, the Pythagorean Archytas of Tarentum, a friend and collaborator of Plato, is known in science for, among other things, as I have reported above, the method for an exact doubling of the cube by no means other than purely geometric construction. This case, of Archytas's doubling of the cube, has exceptional importance for defining the directly internal connection between the ancient Greek experimental science developed on the basis of original discoveries datable to earlier than the construction of the great pyramids of Giza in Egypt, which occurred about 5,000 years ago.

The study of Archytas's doubling of the cube, and of the notable attempts by other ancients, became a focus of attention during the first half of Sixteenth-Century modern Europe, by Italian mathematicians Cardano, et al. The attempt to give algebraic values for the geometric construction presented the mathematicians with what some Eighteenth-Century Leibniz-haters regarded as "impossible," or "imaginary" numbers. The error of leading Eighteenth-Century European mathematicians, most notably d'Alembert, Euler, and Lagrange, on the subject of these "imaginary" numbers which had been presented earlier by Cardano et al., prompted Gauss's revolutionary refutation of the empiricist methods of d'Alembert, Euler, and Lagrange (and, also, implicitly, Cauchy and others later), in Gauss's 1799 doctoral dissertation, which featured Gauss's first definition of The Fundamental Theorem of Algebra.

The importance of pointing to these ancient-to-modern connections here, is that Gauss's devastating attack on the blunders in scientific method by Euler et al., led to the reaffirmation of Gottfried Leibniz's principle of the infinitesimal calculus, or what is otherwise known as Leibniz's universal principle of physical least action. The treatment of problems of the class so clarified by Gauss, and by notables such as Abel, Dirichlet, and Riemann, solved, at least in a very large degree, the most important of the fundamental problems of modern physical science, and, therefore, also modern economy. The subject of this series of progressive developments,

was the necessary physical meaning of the notion of the complex domain.

For the reasons respecting the limitations of simple sense-perception which I broadly indicated above, those objects which are properly classed as uniquely, experimentally defined universal physical principles, such as Kepler's discovery of universal gravitation, Leibniz's discovery of the deeper physical significance of the catenary function, and the related matter of natural logarithms, belong to a class of physically efficient universal physical principles, principles whose existence is not directly accessible by the senses. Thus, in experimental physical science, we encounter the existence of experimentally undeniable such universal physical principles, for which no direct, sensory representation is mathematically possible. That is the physical significance, as opposed to all attempted Cartesian treatments, of the mathematical complex domain for all functions which are experimentally real.

These reflections, by the greatest anti-reductionist European scientists of the Seventeenth through Nineteenth Centuries, culminated in what is most efficiently recognized as a Riemannian anti-Euclidean, rather than a merely non-Euclidean, physical geometry. That is the mathematical physics on which a realization of the objectives of Vladimir I. Vernadsky's treatments of the subjects of the Biosphere and Noösphere depends. Vernadsky's recasting of the problem of what he defines as the Noösphere, is the most appropriate standpoint for discussion and development of my discoveries and related work in the field of the Leibnizian science of applied physical economy.

Reflection on the historical development in science which I have just so summarized here, takes us directly to the proper understanding of the meaning of *powers* in Egyptian and pre-Aristotle Classical ancient Greek physical science. It is the same meaning of powers, which distinguishes the actual discovery of universal gravitation, by Johannes Kepler, from the *push me-beat me-pull me* doctrines of empiricists such as Galileo and the Cartesian current generally. Kepler showed, for the relationship between the orbits of Mars and Earth, that the cause of the motion of the planet could not be defined by any continuous algebraic function, since the motion along the elliptical pathway was predetermined by three distinct gross factors: the continuously non-uniform motion of the planet in its pre-assigned orbital pathway, the singularity expressed by the illusory apparent back-looping within the Mars orbit, relative to an Earth observer, and the fact that the rate of orbiting always conformed to a principle of "equal areas, equal times" relative to the area swept as a sector defined relative to the Sun's position at one of the two foci of the elliptical orbit. Kepler's more fully developed treatment of the principle of gravitation in the Solar System was given a more crucial proof by the way in which Gauss later proved the Keplerian orbit for elements of an exploded planet formerly lying between the orbits of Mars and Jupiter, for the asteroid Ceres.

This brings us to a crucial point about astronomy and other physical science which is an essential principle of any competent science of physical economy. That point is, that, for Kepler, universal gravitation, as expressed by the orbit of a planet, was an *intention* of the Creator, not a mathematical formula in reductionist kinematics. Kepler, like Leibniz after him, was thus echoing the precedent of an ancient Egyptian astronomy, dating from a time prior to the construction of the great pyramids of Giza, and that in a stunningly insightful way. The full meaning of this point could not be grasped by modern European science until the appearance of that 1854 habilitation dissertation which presented the world the essential basis for an anti-Euclidean physical geometry, "On the Hypotheses Which Underlie Geometry."[30] Riemann eliminated all of the formal definitions, axioms, and postulates of any formal Euclidean or non-Euclidean geometry at a single stroke. Without that, it would not have been possible for modern classroom teaching of mathematical physics to have provided students with a competent understanding of what the Pythagoreans signified by the notion of *powers*, or Kepler's introduction of the notion of *intention*, rather than the reductionist's mathematical formulas, as the necessary usage of the term "universal physical principle."

A universal physical principle, as the English translation of Kepler employs the term "intention," is the quality of idea which displaces all notions of a-prioristic definitions, axioms, and postulates from the practice of physical science. It is only as we ban all such reductionists' assumptions, as Riemann carries forward the thrust of the preceding work in this direction, of such as Cusa, Leonardo, Kepler, Leibniz, and, most immediately

Gauss's notion of general physical principles of curvature, as Riemann does in the opening two paragraphs of his 1854 habilitation dissertation, that it becomes possible to express the Classical Egyptian-Pythagorean-Platonic conception of powers forward into that notion's appropriate expression in modern science in general, and in a science of physical economy in particular.[31]

Vernadsky: Three Intentions

The universalist scientific mind of Russian-Ukrainian scientist V.I. Vernadsky, the former student of the great Mendeleyev, and, among numerous other original accomplishments, the author of Soviet nuclear fission technology, returned Russia's (and Ukraine's) science to the founding principles of the Classical, pre-Aristotle science of Thales, the Pythagoreans, and Plato, in his experimentally rigorous discovery of the common principle of what are named the Biosphere and Noösphere.[32]

Vernadsky, trained, like his one-time Professor Mendeleyev, as a physical chemist in the same Russian tradition traced, via Peter the Great, to Saxony's Freiberg Academy, began his attention to the Biosphere from the work of the circles of France's Louis Pasteur et al. Unlike Ludwig Boltzmann's Erwin Schrödinger, who bungled the matter with a reductionist's attempt to explain "life" as a matter of aperiodic crystallization,[33] Vernadsky redefined the universe in terms of the method of Bernhard Riemann, as composing a domain generated by three distinct, multiply-connected principles: the abiotic, the living, and the *noëtic* (the creative principle expressed as the distinction of the human mind from that of all lower forms of life).

In other words, Vernadsky's crucial-experimentalist

---

30. Bernhard Riemann, *Über die Hypothesen, welche der Geometrie zu Grunde liegen*, in **Bernhard Riemanns gesammelte mathematische Werke** (New York: Dover Publications reprint edition, 1953), pp. 272-287.

31. For the scientist, in particular, it is important that my argument on this point here be adopted as the intention of the famous aphorism of Heraclitus, as this is reflected, notably, in Plato's attack on the Eleatics, in the **Parmenides** dialogue. This should also be recognized as Riemann's intention in his usage of "hypotheses," as congruent with the referenced special use of "intention" in my argument on the significance of *powers* here. It is also the underlying implication of the attack on the theology of Aristotle by Philo of Alexandria. It is the rebuke to the famous aphorism uttered by Goethe's Mephistopheles in Auerbach's cellar: "In the beginning was the act." In truth, as in Riemannian anti-Euclidean physical geometry, "In the beginning is the intention," the continually creative form known to the Pythagoreans as "power." This is the essentially underlying principle of the science of physical economy, as Leibniz intended, and as I do, as Vernadsky did.

32. Cf. Lyndon H. LaRouche, Jr., **The Economics of the Noösphere**, op. cit.

33. Erwin Schrödinger, **What Is Life?** (Cambridge: Cambridge University Press, 1992 reprint edition).

methods of laboratory investigations, defined the universe as composed of the interaction among three general types of universal physical principles, of which two are the successively higher-ranking principles of life and human (and God's) creative reason: hence man defined, apart from the beasts, as in the likeness of the Creator. Thus, for Vernadsky, et al., these three, thus ordered by the strictest standards of experimental physics, as multiply-connected, universal physical principles: an explicitly Riemannian universe.

As if to prevent an ingenue's wild-eyed rush into lunatic forms of mysticism, Vernadsky presented such a view of the ongoing developmental process of organization of the physical universe on the proverbial "solid ground" of the evidence of the process of formation, accumulation, and functioning of fossils.[34]

Thus, our planet's personal history is written largely in the shifting composition of the combined growth of three classes of fossils. First, materials which have been developed by "inorganic" processes since the Earth's original material was spun out of the irradiated plasma of the younger Sun, and the material "fractionally distilled" into the Earth's orbit condensed, as Gauss indicated this must have occurred within a Keplerian Solar system, into the planet Earth and its Moon. Second, materials accumulated as fossils of life, including oceans and atmosphere. Third, materials accumulated as products of the action of the human mind, rather than as fossils of living processes.

The commonplace inability of even many well-trained scientists today, to understand the plain intentions of the most accomplished scientists of known history, as I experienced this crippling intellectual fault among even some talented scientists then associated with my celebrated Fusion Energy Foundation of the 1970s and 1980s, could be traced to the oftentimes hysterical defense of the incompetent, but widely taught assumptions of empiricist/positivist dogmas, such as those of Euler, Lagrange, Cauchy, et al., taught as preconditions for certification of scientists in doctoral and other university programs still today. The nature of that shortcoming among them was made clear in comparing the outstanding achievements of some among these scientists, as experimentalists, compared with the sometimes even pathetic attempts at explaining their experimental accomplishments at the mathematics blackboard.

Such behavior among scientists crippled by those induced formalists' habits, was, obviously, nonetheless a more dignified folly than the sheer babbling insanity of the typical leading economists and their like today, particularly the present generation of economists responsible for the lunatic babble which has shaped U.S. economic policy of practice over more than forty years to date. The latter, such as the virtual "wind-up-toy"-like devotees of Siena's Mundell, are clearly more lunatic, more purely, and dangerously stupefied, and thus virtually more brain-dead intellectually, than the most intellectually sterile of nose-picking minds among Soviet economists of the Plekhanov-Kautsky-Bukharin "objective theory of history" school.

To nail down the absolutely crucial point in the argument I am making here, consider the case of Heraclitus. Could Heraclitus have said that? If so, what could he have meant? Is our answer to those questions merely supposition, or is there some available method by which we might show that the statement, as understood by Plato, is of the unique validity we would properly assign to the experimentally validatable, reported discovery of a universal physical principle. (My relevant motto is: Never make a bold assertion of a contentious point on a matter of principle, unless you are already prepared to ambush the objection of the "usual suspects" among your would-be "critics.")

On the subject of the answer to that question concerning Heraclitus, we have two essential starting-points for proof that Heraclitus might have said that;

---

34. This is the setting for demonstration of the superior capability of the present-day Russian and other scientists who continue the legacy of Vernadsky, for providing the world as a whole with essential methods of work, for creating the policies needed for successful long-term management of the world's natural mineral resources. To leave such elements of global policy-shaping to those who have failed to recognize the implications of the Mendeleyev-Vernadsky legacy's grasp of the notion of the Noösphere would surely lead toward a global catastrophe for the human species generally. As I emphasized to relevant elements of the U.S. Reagan Administration, and others, in my proposal for what became President Reagan's Strategic Defense Initiative of March 23, 1983, it would be a tragic mistake, still today, to assess Russia's scientific capabilities from the standpoint of the wretched performance of the Soviet civilian economy. The Soviet system's Marxist ideology, especially what soon proved to be its so-called "objective," but ultimately fatal, reductionists' antipathy toward the "idealistic" methods of Plato, wrecked the performance of the Soviet economy, but Russia's most competent scientists, who, by definition, are Platonic idealists in their methods of work, were often even seemingly "instinctively" superior, given their conditions of work, to scientific methods then, and still, popular in universities of Europe and the U.S.A. In physical science and economics, the refusal to grasp the relevance of Gauss's 1799 attack on the incompetence of d'Alembert, Euler, and Lagrange, is proof in principle that the present-day academic in question was mugged by "brain-washers" on the way to pick up his degree.

that, in any case, what is attributed to him conforms to Plato's exposure of the incompetence of the Eleatic school of Parmenides, et al.; and that Plato's defense of the aphoristic statement attributed to Heraclitus conforms precisely to the arguments and experimental successes of the Pythagorean school.

Notably, as a matter of cross-reference, Plato's view of the relevance of Heraclitus's argument conforms to the later attack on the epistemological incompetence of Aristotle's theology by Philo of Alexandria.[35] The point in all relevant cases, is that Creation of the universe is a continuing process, not the finished effect which the fraudulent Aristotelean method of Claudius Ptolemy proposes. A universal physical principle is not a mathematical projection of the generation of a mathematically precalculated, completed effect within an a-prioristic Aristotelean-Euclidean domain; it is a constantly, universally acting, continuing action of change, as shown by Kepler's discovery of universal gravitation.

It is from this standpoint, that the assumptions underlying the American System of political-economy must be understood and implemented, now on a global scale.

Physical Economy As Such

A competently scientific insight into economy, is derived from an original, primary emphasis on physical economy, without consideration of money or its derivatives as an included functional factor taken into consideration. It is to be emphasized, in opposition to all of the customary nonsense taught in academic courses and textbooks on economy, that, contrary to the babbling insanity of von Neumann's and Morgenstern's *The Theory of Games & Economic Behavior*,[36] for example, there is no self-evident function of money, there is no self-evident sort of definitional treatment of money to be found in the real universe, but only in the effects produced as symptoms of the unreality of certain troubled, or even very, very sick minds.

The original American System of political-economy, was based principally upon the influence of Leib-

niz upon leading circles around the scientist-statesman Benjamin Franklin who, among other things, actually organized the foundations of the Industrial Revolution in mid-Eighteenth-Century England.

The relevant problem which the historian, the late H. Graham Lowry reported to me, during a visit to me by him and his wife in 1983, was that, although we had a mass of evidence showing the influence of Leibniz on the development of the leading American thought which laid the foundations for the American Revolution and our original economic system, we had yet to pin down the original link to leading circles in North America, a link which must be located during the reign of England's Queen Anne and the vast Leibniz network which existed also in the British Isles, as also on the continent of Europe at that time. His book presents the researches which led him to the discovery of the most crucial part of the answer to that problem.[37] Subsequent historical researches, including those within the continent of Europe, have greatly amplified our present knowledge of the details of these connections.

The popular, variously fraudulent or simply ignorant opinion about the Eighteenth-Century foundations of American Constitutional thought, is based on the childish assumption that the roots of North American thought are to be found in a virtual exclusion of anything but the ideological product of the Anglo-Dutch Liberal ideologies of the late Seventeenth and Eighteenth Centuries. That same foolish mistake has been reinforced by the populist and Marxist currents of the mid-Nineteenth through Twentieth Centuries, which trace the birth of British Liberal political-economy almost to the doorstep of Abraham's house in Ur, or, more likely, the Tower of Babel.

Thus, the arrogant ass, and Bertrand Russell acolyte von Neumann traces the birth of economy back to the solitary speculations of Daniel Defoe's fictional Robinson Crusoe, who is fancied as creating the original act of trade by meeting a castaway named "Friday" on their solitary island. Marx, trained at the British Museum under the British Foreign Office's Urquhart, the corresponding coordinator of Lord Palmerston's network of recruits to Giuseppe Mazzini's Young Europe network, was nurtured in nothing so much as the dogmas produced by the sundry inmates of Jeremy Bentham's British East India Company Haileybury School. Marxist economics was never anything but a branch of the Brit-

---

35. Some theologians suffering from a defective education in scientific method, would object to my argument here as containing an implicitly "Gnostic" presumption. That would be an error of the type attributable to indoctrination of some theologians in the actually Gnostic dogma of the reductionists, theologians who implicitly uphold the actual Gnostic dogma by locating the Creator outside the real universe, as the targets of Philo's attack do.

36. 3rd edition, (Princeton: Princeton University Press, 1953)

37. Op. cit.

ish Foreign Office's product, the teaching faithfully followed by a mass of those so-called Marxists and others, who, unlike the exceptional Rosa Luxemburg, had no significant knowledge of any form of economy existing outside the bounds of British political theology.

So, aided by the Cambridge systems analysis pack, still in the halls and latrines of academia today, the world of ideas outside the mythical ideological conflict between British conservatives and the British left is assumed simply not to exist—except for privileged circles who may chuckle knowingly about this popular foolishness out of hearing of the so-called mainstream press. The mythical wars of "right versus left" are the proverbial Alpha and Omega of what passes, in public latrines and elsewhere, for conventional political and economic wisdom. Not to disturb the credulities of the locals, so to speak. What is generally taught and believed about modern economy in most academic and political circles of the world today, is approximately on the same level of intellectual product as the worst popular science-fiction trash. As the 2000 collapse of the United States' "IT bubble" should have reminded people who ought to have known better beforehand, a society whose university-educated types respect the views on economy of John von Neumann and his dupes could not be considered entirely sane.

So, to speak kindly, the imbecility of the current Bush Administration on the subject of economy (among many other matters) can not be blamed entirely upon the inmates of that peculiar institution. Taking into account the fact that good products of all kinds have been driven from the shelves of the principal markets, the product which public opinion appears to prefer, nonetheless does attest somewhat to the current mental condition of that public itself.

The idea that money "earns" a gain for the real economy by, so to speak, just sitting there, is an example of the kind of sheer delusion by which popular belief has conspired to bankrupt what was once the world's leading, and proudest producer society, the U.S.A. That delusion goes with the rumor that organized crime is what brings improvements to the local economy which it loots.

The fact is that the most intellectual species of higher ape, left without man on our planet, could never have achieved a current living population of more than several millions at any time during the periods of oscillating ice ages during the past two millions years or so. Curiously, there are more than six billions living per-

sons counted on this planet today. Why was the Earth's human population no more than about ten percent of that level back during the Fourteenth Century? Because the level of practiced technology did not permit a significantly higher level back during a century when the population of Europe collapsed by a net amount of about thirty percent during that century's New Dark Age. The difference between ape and man is the human mind's creative powers, those powers expressed by what Vernadsky defined as the Noösphere: not money, saved, invested, or otherwise.

In fact, the need for the role of money arises out of the fact, that the creative powers of the human species are concentrated, as perfectly sovereign, noëtic powers of the individual human mind. There is no creative intelligence floating around in the cracks between people, nor can it be extracted from digital computers. Nor does money function essentially as a means of trade among people. The most essential function of money in modern society is the formation of medium- to long-term physical-capital investments in the improvement of the productive powers of labor of society as a whole.

Know-it-alls who are ignorant of the ABCs of real economy, think "capital" means financial capital. Real capital is physical capital, which must be defined in meaning by standards of measure which do not directly involve the notion of money.

For example, as I have insisted in sundry other published locations, if the U.S.A. is to resume a long-neglected useful function for the world at large, a mission orientation which the U.S. would have adopted at the close of the last great war, but for the untimely death of President Franklin Roosevelt, we must now take into account the pressing needs of the population of regions such as Asia for a chiefly postponed, rapid influence of technological improvements in both the circumstances of life and means of production to lift the masses of Asia, within not less than two generations (e.g., fifty years) up to a truly self-sustaining level. This requires the mobilization of resources on the front-end of scientific and technological progress from around the world as a whole, including Europe, the Americas, and Asia generally.

Much of this contribution must be supplied from the U.S.A. and Europe. This requires the adoption of a mission-orientation for the culture of Europe and North America, which must include the specification that we require a labor-force which reaches the level of competence of a scientific or comparable profession by about the age of twenty-five; a quarter-century. This translates as a twenty-five year investment in the future productive powers of the U.S. population.

All important capital cycles, are, in fact, cycles of the lifetime of physical-capital improvements, cycles for physical capital which must be measured as ratios of the physical lifetime of that investment to the quarter-century, for example, required to produce a qualified U.S. scientist or equivalent professional today.

The sane notion of profit and its function, is therefore to be derived from the rate of increase of gain in productivity of nations and their labor-forces through scientific and technological progress, including the effects of investment in the postponed consumption represented by physical-capital investments in basic economic infrastructure, and particular enterprises.

These relations are most readily defined by proceeding from the standpoint of Vernadsky's conception of physical economy, or, what may be otherwise defined as a neo-Leibnizian approach to physical economy. There is nothing in Leibniz's net work on the subject of economy, which does not anticipate the implications of Vernadsky's thought for the world of today. There is, therefore, no inconsistency between Vernadsky's approach to economy and that of U.S. Treasury Secretary Alexander Hamilton's 1791 Report to the U.S. Congress *On the Subject of Manufactures*. Junk the hoaxster and plagiarist Adam Smith, junk the evil Jeremy Bentham and his crew. Send Karl Marx back to school to learn real economics, for a change. The connection of Leibniz to Vernadsky, defined in respect to the notion of physical economy, is the happy future of our world.

We must manage this planet, and, more and more, our Solar System as well. We must attend to the ratio of increase of abiotic fossils to the mass of the planet as a whole. We must attend to the improvement of the ratio of the fossils and active portion of the Biosphere to the planet as a whole, and to the abiotic fossil domain. We must increase, more rapidly than all the rest, the fossil products of the Noösphere.

To this end, we must regulate the creation and circulation of money, as the protectionist tradition of the U.S.A. has been the root of all periods of great improvement in the productive powers of labor of the U.S.A. economy as a whole. What President Franklin Roosevelt and his Administration did, in protectionist measures to save the U.S. from the collapse which a reelection of Hoover would have assured, were not innovations contrary to our original Federal Constitution, but changes, partly improvisations required by emergency,

of a type which should have been the common practice of our republic from its birth, the intention of the original Constitution, had we had the circumstances and will to do that under the aversive conditions imposed upon us by the menacing lunacy which took over Europe from July 1789 on.

Money is an idiot which attracts idiots more than anyone else. Therefore, money must be regulated, so that it serves the mission, of promoting needed forms of *physical-capital formation*, physical improvement in the productive powers of labor through technological progress, and high rates of physical-economic growth, especially in the increase of the productive powers of labor through scientific and cultural advances. The idea of the lending of money as a source of "natural profit" of an economy is usury, a dangerous mental illness whose spread must be prevented by the only agency which should ever be permitted to create money, the government of a sovereign republic.

4. Bringing Asia Into the System

Consider the great obstacle to global remedies which the behavior of Anglo-Dutch Liberalism has built up within Asia, over recent centuries. I mean, most emphatically, the imposition upon Asia, among other places, of disregard for the difference between man and human cattle, a disregard which is characteristic of the empiricist and derived philosophical world-outlooks.

Although the modern science and technology which European civilization did, admittedly, introduce to subjugated regions of Asia and Africa (for example), were a source of means for great improvements in the productive powers of labor, and related potential improvements in life-expectancy in affected places, even where such opportunities were provided, these putative benefits had more often the character of an externally imposed, rather than self-developed improvement in the relevant national cultures.

My subject here, in this conclusion of my report, toward which I have been leading until now, is the urgency of promoting among both Asians and non-Asians alike, an informed sense of those means of self-development needed to establish the kind of understanding needed for a permanent community of fruitful cooperation among what we may distinguish today as the natural successor to the intent of the 1648 Treaty of Westphalia: a community of sovereign nations dedicated to

CCTV

China's Shenzhou spacecraft after its return from an unmanned test in 1999.

promote, each, the advantage of the other.

In the awful alternative to that urgently needed reform by treaty agreement among sovereigns, if the modern tradition of the empiricists were continued, the doom of planetary civilization were now assured, given circumstances exemplified by the lunatic obscenity of those Bush Administration policies which are already ongoing in Iraq and aimed for other targeted areas.

Given, the arguments on the matter of European civilization and its own historically defined internal problems, how shall we then understand the problems which European civilization has fostered, in one way or another in Asia, for example? How can we bring nations together for durable long-term treaty-agreements of the needed kind, if we have not established the common principle upon which the possibility of such agreements depends?

The answer some Europeans and others would offer, in response to that question, might be the following.

The disgusting feature of most of the expressions of purported good intentions toward the relevant regions of Asia and Africa today, is that what has been extended to the populations of this regions, has been the tradition of what some less insightful critics of that history might describe as the training of the relatively few in the qualifications for being colonial house-servants of the Anglo-Dutch Liberal empire. Those critics would probably argue, that, only rarely, does an Asian or African observer perceive some sense of what might be called the secrets of the rise of European civilization to its leading, but lately declining role as, not merely a world physical power, but also that role of a leading world cultural power which was abused by the colonial powers to achieve their presently continuing imperial status of overlordship.

Those, or similar criticisms of colonial and kindred past practice toward Asia and Africa, might be well-meaning, but the critics would argue differently if they could be truthful to themselves about themselves, and about the history of their own cultures.

The fact is, that, lately, especially during the past four decades, what the Anglo-Dutch and related powers have done to Asia is largely an imitation, in effect, of what we, in Europe and the U.S.A., in particular, have done to the generation which is occupying most of the leading positions of power in our own nations, the generation of young adults we ruined culturally, in Europe and the Americas, during the recent forty years. The worst things we have done to the cultures of Asia today, are the things we, in Europe and the Americas, have done, at the same time, to ourselves.

The problem is, that the Anglo-Dutch Liberal interests never had a policy of affording the people of Asia, for example, access to the kinds of knowledge and experience on which the greatest achievements of European culture had depended, the kind of knowledge and experience which I have emphasized in the preceding sections of this report.

The death of President Franklin Roosevelt, now that the threat of a German fascist empire had been eliminated, gave the Anglo-Dutch Liberal component of Trans-Atlantic oligarchical power the opportunity, to rid themselves, as rapidly as possible of their most deadly ancient enemy, the American System rooted in the great Classical tradition of Solon of Athens, et al. With the aid of a state of terror, led by the accomplices of Winston Churchill and President Harry S Truman, instruments of Satanic decadence, such as the Congress for Cultural Freedom, were used to break the will of the majority of the people of the U.S.A., as I personally observed this first-hand as it was happening. The same was done, by the same existentialist cult in Europe, both against the Classical cultural tradition in Europe, and to corrupt the anti-Communist opposition in the Soviet Union and the portions of eastern Europe occupied by Soviet forces.

Consider the relevance of the influence of the satanic Bertrand Russell, in his dual capacity as the principal proponent of world government through the terror of so-called preventive nuclear warfare, and. at the same time, the corruption of morals and science by the spread of anti-Classical dogma in forms such as the work of Norbert Wiener and John von Neumann. Consider the left-wing version of existentialist fascism associated with Berthold Brecht, Theodor Adorno, Hannah Arendt, Herbert Marcuse, et al. The image of the self-destruction of the economy and morals of transatlantic post-1946 culture is typified, summarily, by the putrid smell of the spread of the existentialist, implicitly Brechtian cult of Regie Theater in Germany, combined with assistance from the evil roles of Arthur Burns and High Commissioner John J. McCloy.

From 1945 on, it was the intent of the Anglo-Dutch Liberal establishment to destroy what the U.S.A. under the leadership of Franklin, Washington, Hamilton, Lincoln, and Roosevelt had represented. Its intent then was to destroy the U.S.A. and what it represented internationally, by, first, destroying this legacy in the U.S.A. itself. The generation born after the close of the war, the generation which marched into universities during the middle through late 1960s, were designed, by help of instruments of influence such as the Congress for Cultural Freedom, to induce the U.S.A. and western Europe to destroy their own culture and morals, as the indispensable prerequisite for establishing that new guise of Anglo-Dutch Liberal imperialism identified as "globalization" today.

Thus, the cultural problem of Asia today, is not what the U.S.A. and imperial Britain are taking away from Asia. The cultural problem of Asia, is, chiefly, Asia's imitation of what the U.S.A. and Britain have done to themselves, especially over the course of the recent forty years.

That is the truth about the character and effects of the culture which the Anglo-Dutch Liberal establishment is intent upon imposing upon Asia and also Africa today.

There are also, long-standing cultural problems which have been added to the effects of the more recent efforts to effect the combined self-destruction of the cultures of the world as a whole.

The generic expression of that problem is to be found in the matters which have been emphasized in the course of the preceding sections of this report: that a simply super-imposed culture, whatever its presumably offsetting benefits, is a tragedy. It is a policy of practice which is contrary to the essential nature of the human species. It is policy rooted not only in the predicates of the morally and formally-intellectually defective empiricist way of reductionist thinking. It is evil, in and of itself; it is evil which engenders evil.

Therefore, the thesis to be pursued now is this: *Imposition of standards of cultural sanity, is not tyranny, is not the cause of the problems of Asia today. The chief source of corruption in Asia culture today, is the attempt to rival the present forms of cultural decadence prevalent in European culture's leading circles of today. This kind of corruption of Asian culture, combined with the hatred engendered through the grievances caused by European abuses, tends to prevent the cultures of Asia and Africa from discovering the deeper roots of their present problem within Asian, or African culture itself. On this account, Asian patriots must study the history of European civilization more carefully, to see what universal principles are demonstrated, for both European and Asian cultures today, by tracing the internal struggles between right and wrong, in European history, down to the epistemological roots of that conflict. This must be done for the purpose, that Asia might not repeat, in its own way, the kind of folly which sent ancient Classical Greece down to its own self-inflicted defeat.*

As to certain, actually rather irrelevant criticisms of the culture of the U.S. and Europe from Asia: There is nothing wrong, but quite the contrary, in certain imposed changes in culture of a people. Such as the outlawing of cannibalism, the outlawing of crimes against the Jews such as the tradition of Grand Inquisitor Tomás de Torquemada as maintained by Adolf Hitler's attempted genocide against the Jews, or the outlawing of the death-penalty in contemporary civilized forms of society. If the culture so modified were evil, or even simply defective, that aspect of the intention were justified. However, the moral judgment to be passed upon what is done in service of that avowed intention, depends not on the intent as such, but upon the way in which the change is brought about. What the British did in India, is an example of the problem. What Palmerston, Bertrand Russell, et al. did to China, is an example of the crime.

There is nothing arbitrary in the set of rules which I have thus just stated or implied. In the matter of change, what is crucial is the morality of the choice of method by which an otherwise justifiable goal is attained. The correct method for improvement of a culture, is the Socratic method of Plato, et al. The use of any contrary method, except as the prevention of a crime such as Torquemada's, is itself a crime.

Some things are, indeed, universally true, or as universally true as what is absolutely true for a certain time and place in the history of mankind as a whole. The crucial thing is to recognize, and respond to the distinctions to be taken into account. How can one propose to enforce the principle of truth, if knowledge of the truth is prevented, as under the doctrines of law practiced inside the U.S.A. today? How can there be knowledge of the truth, when the practice of truth as policy and law is evaded? How can there be honesty in a culture which practices the moral relativism of the typical modern academic cultural anthropologist? For example, cannibalism is simply wrong, and cannabis-ism is not much better. Mass murder through the effects of the influence of irrationalist "environmentalist" cults, is a crime of willful mass murder. Murder in the name of God is still Satanism, however devout the practice.

What, therefore, these points considered, should we signify by "the consent of the governed?" Simplistic popular rules of so-called "right and wrong" are a practice of the cruel ignorance of barbarians. What, better than such traditionalist forms of moralizing populist rubbish, should be what we could rightly signify as "the adequately informed consent of the governed"? There, in the term "adequately informed," the challenge of Asia today comes to the fore. The principles of scientific discovery which I have stressed in the foregoing chapters have been intended to prepare us, now, for looking at remedies for the plight of Asia's future prospects today.

The Difference Within European Culture

The empiricists' attempts to define European culture, European habits, and so on, as if statistically, are to be brushed aside as obvious sophistry. Man is a creature whose cultures have always been in internal conflict. The truth of the matter of any culture as a whole, lies in recognizing the difference between what has been true, and what has been false in the contested policies of the conflicted factional currents of that culture, as Schiller's contrast of the legacy of Solon to that of Lycurgus illustrates the point for the case of ancient Greece and its legacy for modern times. Thus, the attacks on "European culture" by some Asians, are a sophistry as absurd, and as corrupting as anything encountered from "the West."

The best achievement of European culture has been the impact of a discovery of that conscious implementation of that principle of hypothesis made famous through the dialogues of Plato. A focus of attention on the obstacles to such a view of that matter from Asia, is the pivotal positive issue of concern in this report. That lack of a clear perspective on this question, is the greatest single obstacle today, in the urgently needed attempt to establish the management of the planet by a concert of sovereign nation-states which, together, represents a true, rather than arbitrary Eurasian cultural paradigm.

Another way of defining the approach to be taken to that end, is a closer examination of the relationship between Russia and India. Russia's character has been its development as an exemplary development of an Eurasian culture. For this reason, although relations between India and Russia are not always easy ones, the Eurasian character specific to India itself, has made the prospect of a cooperation among Eurasian nations which is built around the keystone of Russia-India-China cooperation, for me the obvious pivotal goal of an informed U.S.A. self-interest in foreign policy, since the 1970s, a goal which has gained greatly in importance, in my estimation, since the period of U.S. President Clinton's tenure. Now, we have entered a time when the saving of the economy of western and central Europe depends pivotally upon long-term economic cooperation between continental European economy and a Russia-India-China-pivotted Eurasian concert. When we consider the shortfalls and advantages distributed among the prospective partners to such long-term economic collaboration, the successful establishment of a network of long-term treaty-agreements based upon a Eurasian perspective is of the utmost urgency.

The realization of such hopes, requires a radical shift in Europe and the U.S.A., the former hotbeds of science-driven technological progress, back to their proper long-term, actually vitally self-interest roles as the principal engine of the benefits of global scientific and technological progress for the planet as a whole. However, presuming that we are able to use the presently onrushing general collapse of the present world monetary-financial system, to establish a new arrangement not inconsistent with the best features of the 1944-1964 Bretton Woods system, the challenge will be to develop within Asian nations a growing habit of emulating the best examples of Classical scientific and cultural progress from the history of European civilization, especially the role of such scientific and cultural progress unleashed by Europe's Fifteenth-Century Renaissance: the legacy of Cusa, Leonardo, Kepler, Leibniz, Gauss, Riemann, and Vernadsky.

That challenge should focus attention by Asians on the issues which I have emphasized in the earlier chapters of this report. This means, for example, freeing India's culture from the grip of corrupting softness toward the imperial design, which is embedded in all of the sundry elements of the Fabian schemes associated with the names of H.G. Wells and Bertrand Russell. The tendency for vacillation between oriental mysticism and radical forms of reductionism in science, is typical of the cultural influence which had tended to constrict the ration of qualified scientific thinkers, qualified in physical science, rather than formal mathematics, among the educated strata of Asia. The special importance of this factor in Asia during the recent nearly sixty years in general, and the recent forty years more emphatically, is that this lack of a broadly developed Classical, anti-reductionist culture of science in Asia intersects the moral and intellectual degeneration of European ideas and practices in science and culture during the recent forty years.

Thus, Asia has lacked the spirit of competition with European scientific progress, that, in significant part, because of the willful drying out of the well-springs of a Classical scientific and artistic culture in Europe and the Americas themselves, during these recent four decades, most emphatically. The want of the Asian's sense of the need to compete in these domains which are no longer regarded seriously in the practice of the U.S.A. and Europe itself, dulls the sensibilities among Asians, by implying that competition requires they should match European and U.S. performance, under conditions in which the relevant European standards have been degenerating catastrophically.

The consequence of a certain dullness respecting this ugly correlation of trends, is that we are producing a vast expansion of the population of Asia, but failing to absorb the great majority of that population in the forms of cultural development needed to assure the survival of those nations during the generation immediately ahead. This deadly infection has been accompanied by a "get rich" fanaticism spread among relevant strata of educated Asians, a kind of "get rich" obsession which has always been, in history, the hallmark, as in the U.S.A. of the recent three decades, of a culture moving toward the brink of a self-induced physical as much as moral collapse.

In short, the issues of creativity which I have emphasized in the preceding chapters, point to the most deadly of the threats, including self-inflicted, immediate threats, to the nations of Asia today.

Probably, Bal Gangadhar Tilak, for example, would have understood me.

The 'Orion' Concept

The moral degeneracy of English language morals from the high standard typified by the work of Sir Thomas More and William Shakespeare, can be dated in a most relevant way from the influence of the Venetian Party empiricists as expressed through the roles of Sir Francis Bacon and Thomas Hobbes. What prompted Bacon's circles to drive Shakespeare from the stage, to make way for silly buffoons, was the same hatred against the practice of Classical irony and metaphor which was expressed by that student of Galileo, Bacon's beloved Thomas Hobbes.

One of the most impressive demonstrations of the relevant point to be made on account of English style in Venetian depravity was Tilak's argument, as in his 1893 *Orion*, respecting the oral transmission of essentially accurate data respecting the Vernal Equinox, in the constellation of Orion, of more than four millennia earlier, conveyed largely by the oral transmission of certain Vedic hymns into modern Sanskrit practice. Virtually no modern editor could ordinarily show either the competence, or even the desire to transmit an accurate account of the actual intent of a passage from even an address delivered yesterday!

It was made clear to me, as by relevant scholars at Pune, that my suspicions as to the source of this Vedic achievement were correct. The answer to the obvious question posed thus, is already available to us from knowledge of the practice of actually Classical forms of modern English (for example) poetry, from a somewhat broader view of the scope of the matter, than was presented by William Empson in his writings on the subject of types of ambiguity. Had Empson amplified his studies to take into account the implications of J.S. Bach's development and employment of well-tempering as such,[38] he would have reached conclusions akin to those I shared with Pune scholars on the matter of the

---

38. As the LaRouche Youth Movement has encountered the depth of Bach's method in its work seeking to master the conceptual requirements, of ideas, for the performance, in the mandatory *bel canto* mode, of even a single work, Bach's ***Jesu, meine Freude*** motet.

remarkable fidelity in the transmission of these Vedic hymns to modern times.

The damnable fraud of Hobbes and his followers is exemplary of the reasons, rooted in empiricism, for the failure of the ability to use language for conveying actual ideas in relevant parts of the putatively educated populations of Europe and the Americas today.

All competent development and transmission of true knowledge can occur only in the mode associated with an attempt at a perfected mastery of the set of Plato's Socratic dialogues. The examination of these dialogues against the background of Thales, fragments of Heraclitus, Solon, and the Pythagoreans such as Archytas, must be seen as touching the same point which is crucially implicit in Empson's attempted treatments of the subject of irony. That exercise must be complemented by the study of the implications of the well-tempered performance, at C=256, of Bach's choral works. The best efforts of that vanishing tribe, the Classical artists of the Classical stage, is of great importance in the process of educating young people to the level of mastering the implications of Classical ambiguity as a matter of their own independent knowledge.

This feature, of the role of Classical irony in poetry, music, and drama, expresses the same principle met in the original discovery of experimentally validated universal physical principles, as I have stressed this point in the preceding chapters. It turns our attention back to Tilak's study of the implications of certain Vedic hymns.

Although the ration of the total population in European cultures which has expressed this approach, which I have emphasized in the preceding chapters, has never been more than a tiny fraction of the total population, the role of that tiny fraction has been the crucial margin of difference which led, over many rocky roads and through deadly swamps, into the greatest achievements of modern Classical European scientific and artistic culture; it is that minority which has contributed its indispensable role in setting the pace for the progress and relative power achieved by the Classical modes in European civilization.

Look at this again, this time from the standpoint of a much higher English authority than Empson, Percy Shelley's *A Defence of Poetry*. *There are periods in the history of peoples during which there is an extraordinary increase of the power of imparting and receiving profound and impassioned conceptions respecting man and nature.* This phenomenon, as I have been able to study it closely in the course of my teaching activities, work with leading scientists, and otherwise, has been the driving force of progress for all European civilization since Europe's emergence under the patronage of the most knowledgeable circles of ancient Egypt, the circles which undoubtedly included the Moses of the Moseses.

By aid of my own experience in those climates of my work, it is made obvious to me, that the role of the equivalent of Classical irony, as I have summarily identified that here, is the driving force of progress of cultures, from within cultures. In particular, if we focus on the internal history of the development of European physical science in a Classical mode, over the recent 2,500 and longer years of fairly documented relevant elements of history, we see how Classical forms of ambiguity define the self-development of an entire culture, through the impact of the Classical poets and kindred thinkers of that culture. We see that as this is typified by the best modes and works in poetry, or the similar role of the Platonic form of dialogue in physical science.

What occurs, as I have seen thus often, even at close quarters, in the course of my lifetime, the evolution of the collective mind of an entire culture, is driven by the spark of the interventions into the entire society, through the veil of ambiguity, by a relatively few geniuses, and by those young people who replicate experience of discovery by geniuses in their own early self-development through young adulthood.

The crucial point to be emphasized here, is that the myth of the textbook must be rejected as false. The idea of learning, as if "to repeat after me," the outward form of a discovery, must be ejected from educational and related practices. The individual must re-experience the actual act of discovery, or rediscovery of ideas in the sense that the collected Socratic dialogues of Plato are a map of the only competent mode of general and specialized education, alike. The people of a culture can develop only by avoiding the practice of mere imitation of what is copied from other cultures. What a national culture knows, is what is known through the act of experiencing, or re-experiencing original discoveries of principle in the domains of physical science and Classical culture.

The great, distinguishing accomplishment of European culture, since ancient Greece, has been the cumulative impact of this factor of Classical culture. In all the ebbs and flows of European culture since Solon of Athens wrote his rebuke to the citizens of his state, the continuity of the process of transmission and development was never broken. Witness the clinical behavior of the internal history of European Christianity as a demonstration of that point.

From the beginning of Christianity, as expressed within continental European culture since the mission of the Apostle Peter to Italy, and Paul to Greece and Italy, Christianity has represented, in its essentials, a mode in which that Classical culture of Greece associated with Socrates, Plato, and their relevant forerunners, has been continued to the present day. Inevitably, this aspect of Christianity was treated from the beginning, with the crucifixion of Christ by Tiberius's titular son-in-law Pontius Pilate, as the greatest kind of threat to imperial Rome. Inevitably, the methods of state-sponsored corruption were added to mass-murderous persecution as a Roman commitment to wiping out the actuality of the content of the Apostolic Christianity associated with the Classical Greek implications of the works of the Apostles John and Paul.

The corruption of Christianity through sundry varieties of cults and what-not was cumulatively prodigious. Nonetheless, it survived, and with it, and with the aid of Classical culture transmitted by currents in Judaism and Islam, as in the pre-1492 Iberian peninsula, the essentials of the Greek Classical legacy survived to achieve its resurgence in the Fifteenth-Century, Italy-centered Renaissance.

The transformation of the principal traditional non-Latin languages of Europe, as typified by Dante Alighieri's rescue of Italian from the prison of captor Latin, was associated with a rebirth of these languages into a literate form which was crafted to facilitate the resurgence of the methods of Classical thought. Thus, modern Europe, and, with it, the modern concept of the sovereign nation-state republic, was born during the Fifteenth-Century Renaissance, and that half-suffocated infant resuscitated by the 1648 Treaty of Westphalia.

Thus, despite all else, Classical scientific and related culture has been preserved, and developed further, by a never broken skein of development in the history of European culture since ancient Greece.

In contrast, the manner in which European colonization was conducted, from Iberia, and then in the Anglo-Dutch mode, was intended to prevent the subjugated peoples of the colonization from being the intellectual masters of their own fate, as was the ban on literacy of slaves in the pre-Lincoln U.S.A. pro-slavery states. Although elements of European science, for example, were exported into the Anglo-Dutch regions of European colonization, the basis for the development of that scientific, and related knowledge of principle was effectively suppressed, to the effect that the assimilation of science and related knowledge was not experienced as an integral part of the processes of the cultural development of those captive peoples.

Thus, for example, even the very idea of the sovereign nation-state was adopted as a mimicry, rather than as comprehension of the principle from which the European conception of the modern sovereign nation-state republic had been generated. Compare the processes leading into the Fifteenth-Century European Renaissance, when the first modern nation-states, Louis XI's France and Henry VII's England, were established.

Therefore, in the preceding chapters of this report, I have placed my emphasis on precisely those historically determined differences in the experience of European and Asian cultures. We can not desire to craft some magic recipe for the needed immediate collaboration among Asian and European cultures' states. We must proceed more modestly, using our defense of the principle of national sovereignty as a precaution against attempting to go too far in imposing some arbitrary form of sameness upon peoples.

We must recognize that no people can be functionally sovereign in respect of responsibility for their own peoples' beliefs, except they be perfectly sovereign in their national affairs. This essential function of this sovereignty must be recognized as cultural in essence. To govern themselves, a people must share a common basis in knowledge, which means the development of a national culture in the sense I have defined culture implicitly here. Relations among such states must be in the principled form of a Platonic Socratic dialogue concerning ideas. There are principles of commonality which unite nations in common purpose, but that commonality must be forged in the development of ideas, by national cultures, in dialogue with national cultures.

The principles which stand out as requisite common objectives are chiefly those, such as principles of the science of physical economy, on which I have placed emphasis in the preceding chapters of this report. Any attempt to hasten to what might be premature agreements on other matters, is to be avoided. The process of development of mission-oriented cooperation among the cultures of this planet, must be seen as a continuing process, over generations yet to come. Rather than hastening to the wrong destination, let us learn to enjoy the leisure of journey itself, that to the mutual satisfaction of us all.